Making Beautiful
Beads

metal

glass

fiber

polymer clay

Making
Beautiful
Beads

metal

glass

fiber

polymer clay

EDITOR
Suzanne J. E. Tourtillott

ART DIRECTOR
Susan McBride

COVER DESIGN
Barabara Zaretsky

PHOTOGRAPHY
Evan Bracken

EDITORIAL ASSISTANCE
Veronika Alice Gunter
Natalie Mornu
Rain Newcomb

Library of Congress Cataloging-in-Publication Data

Making beautiful beads: glass, metal, polymer clay, fiber/Suzanne J. E. Tourtillott, editor.
   p. Cm.
   Includes index.
   ISBN 1-57990-433-5
   1. Beadwork. I. Tourtillott, Suzanne J. E.
   TT860.M29 2002
745.58'2–dc21   2001038419

10 9 8 7 6 5 4 3 2 1

Published by Lark Books, a division of
Sterling Publishing Co., Inc.
387 Park Avenue South, New York, N.Y. 10016

First Paperback Edition 2003
© 2002, Lark Books

Distributed in Canada by Sterling Publishing,
c/o Canadian Manda Group, One Atlantic Ave., Suite 105
Toronto, Ontario, Canada M6K 3E7

Distributed in the U.K. by:
Guild of Master Craftsman Publications Ltd.
Castle Place
166 High Street
Lewes
East Sussex
England
BN7 1XU
Tel: (+ 44) 1273 477374
Fax: (+ 44) 1273 478606
Email: pubs@thegmcgroup.com
Web: www.gmcpublications.com

Distributed in Australia by Capricorn Link (Australia) Pty Ltd., P.O. Box 704, Windsor, NSW 2756 Australia

If you have questions or comments about this book, please contact:
Lark Books
67 Broadway
Asheville, NC 28801
(828) 253-0467

Printed in China

ISBN 1-57990-433-5

Making Beautiful Beads: metal, glass, fiber, polymer clay

The Illustrious Bead

Beads have been a part of our lives since the earliest of ancient times, and they've been used in all cultures and for all types of purposes. In their long history, beads have expressed social status, religious beliefs and customs, and even been traded as a form of currency. Archaeological finds have discovered artful beads made from stone, shell, bone, and metal, to name a few of the raw materials used for these lasting treasures. Some beads have even been thought to have magical qualities that can be imparted to the owner. Whether in the strong, simple presence of a few on a strand, or the dazzle of thousands of tiny orbs used as embellishment on cloth or leather, beads have enduring appeal. At some fundamental level, most of us love to collect and use beads, no matter what they're made from.

Making Beautiful Beads takes you right to the beginning of the bead making process. As you read this book, you may be surprised at the wealth of creative ideas the five talented designers have brought to the task of making beads. Their ingenuity, mastery of the medium, and sense of play come through again and again in the beautiful work they've done. Their beads reflect aesthetic influences that range from the high mountains of Tibet to the African plains. And as guest writers, each of these designers presents an introduction to her knowledge of the materials, tools, and techniques—everything you'll need to know to get started—for making beads in glass, metal, felt, paper, and polymer clay.

The chapter on fiber media—with Jorie Johnson's felt beads and Ann Marie Kennedy's paper ones—uses wonderfully simple techniques, and you'll be able to begin at once to create lovely, one-of-a-kind beads. Irene Semanchuk Dean's intriguing polymer clay beads seem to transcend their basic material, often imitating the qualities of various types of stone. Some of Joanna Gollberg's great metal beads can be easily made with a set of "cold" metalworking tools. Finally, Kimberley Adams shows you that almost anyone, with some concentration and a little practice, can make stunning glass beads.

With your creative beads in hand, you can design your own jewelry pieces by reading here about how to select and use the perfect findings, cord, and more. Once you've crafted some of your own, perhaps you'll discover the magical qualities inherent in your own beautiful handmade beads.

—Suzanne Tourtillot, Editor

Introduction to Felt

BY JORIE JOHNSON

Remember those annoying little wool balls you find clinging to your winter sweaters by the end of the season? Well, it may sound funny, but with a little more of the same material—and a great deal more strategy—you can create a series of stunning beads for stringing, buttons, and more!

For a few thousand years, the wool from sheep has been spun into yarn for knitting and weaving, but even before that time wool, in its simplest washed and combed state, was shaped and shrunk into forms in a process called feltmaking. Nomads in Central Asia still use centuries-old techniques for making wool felt for their boots, bags, carpets, and tents or yurts. Not only is wool a simple material that grows back after being sheared from its source, the "supplier," having legs, can actually travel with the felt maker, and therefore wool has been used for survival by nomads throughout the world.

A convenient fact about feltmaking is that it requires relatively little equipment, even to successfully complete the projects in this book. Really the most important tool is your pair of hands; the remaining equipment you can probably find around the home. You may even find out that your pet can supply you with enough fur to make a bead or two! Let's look at what you need to get started.

The Basics

Feltmaking is simple to do because you need very few materials to begin, but the results are really rewarding.

Gathering Wool

There's a great variety of wool available, and it's important to ask for and choose the appropriate quality for the type of project you want to felt. Few of us are nomads these days; luckily, there are plentiful sources out there for brightly dyed, carded, and packaged wool to start off with—before you decide to raise your own "suppliers." If you don't have a sheep or two in the neighborhood, then you'll be buying your wool in the form of wool *top* or wool *batts.* At the factory, wool is washed, dyed, then carded or combed, in order to align the fibers in the same direction, making it ready to spin into yarn. The wool at this stage of preparation is referred to as top and looks like a thick, soft wool rope. Batts of wool are thick sheets of carded wool fibers. Or you can get even closer to the source and buy a fleece,

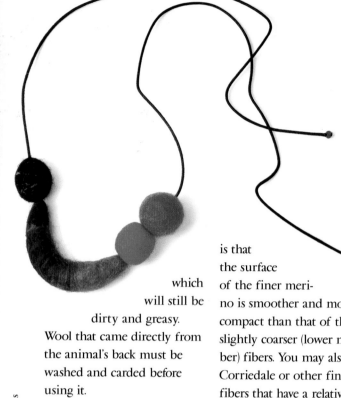

which will still be dirty and greasy. Wool that came directly from the animal's back must be washed and carded before using it.

There is a variety of sheep's wool available for a variety of purposes. Each breed tends to be of a different nature and is raised essentially for either its wool or meat qualities. Even the wool for spinning may be divided into diverse categories, such as those for carpets or for baby clothes. Good quality felting wool is necessary to speed you on your way. *Merino* breed, for example, is probably the best wool for quickly producing small objects.

Merino is available in coarse, medium, and fine quality fibers. The wool sold to factories is graded with a number system that indicates the quality of its fineness: the finer the fiber, the higher the number; 60- to 70-grade works well in bead making. The only difference you may find

is that the surface of the finer merino is smoother and more compact than that of the slightly coarser (lower number) fibers. You may also use Corriedale or other fine wool fibers that have a relatively short fiber length of 2 to 2$^1/_2$ inches (5 to 6.4 cm). It's also possible to cut longer fibers in half, or thirds, which will let them mass together faster.

Why use wool? Appropriate sheep's wool has the highest shrinking capabilities of any in the protein fiber group because each shaft has a special surface structure similar to the way shingles are overlaid on your roof. When you change the condition of the wool fiber by moistening it with a little warm, soapy water, the fiber's scales or cuticles are shocked and tend to expand outward. Then by pushing them around a bit, or massaging them in a certain direction, you can begin to form a shape. Time is also an important factor in feltmaking. For example, if you work on a

basic bead for three minutes and then check its compressibility, it's probably still a bit soft. If you continue working on it for another two to three minutes you'll feel the obvious difference in the firmness of the object.

It's important to experiment for yourself. Gradually you'll learn other lessons about the quality of certain wools from certain suppliers. Although you'll need only a small quantity of wool to begin with, it's certainly best to start off by purchasing a variety pack of colors. It's definitely exhilarating and fun to have an exciting color palette to work with from the start! When first ordering wool, play it safe and explain to the store that you're planning to make felt beads. You need an appropriate wool, such as merino, that will felt quickly and compact well. There are many suppliers worldwide who'll mail-order to you, so you shouldn't have any difficulty locating what you need.

As a simple test, moisten a small amount of tightly rolled, fluffy washed wool with some warm water and soap. Apply a little soap to your palms and, with a circular motion and pressure, start rolling the wool into a spherical shape between the palms of your hands. Within a few minutes you should have something that looks like a ball. Add a little more soap

and warm water, if necessary, and apply more pressure as the fibers begin to mix and mass together. The longer you roll the ball, the harder and smaller it should get. Is it as firm as if you were pinching the tabletop between your fingers? See who among your friends can make the hardest ball. Try bouncing the ball on the table or floor, and you'll soon see that the harder the ball gets, the higher it will bounce (before you start, remember to squeeze out the excess soapy water first!).

The Felting Solution

Hot water helps relax the wool fibers, but it's only when you change their pH condition that it actually causes the fibers to become "alerted" for felting. A felting solution of 1 teaspoon (5 g) of shampoo in 17 to 20 fluid ounces (500 to 600 cc) of warm water should be sufficient to start. Shampoos vary in concentration and will produce varying amounts of suds, depending on the hardness of your local water. You'll need enough suds to slide the fibers around, but not so much that your work area looks like a whipped cream factory. Too much soapsuds means there will be a lot of air between the layers of fibers, which reduces the contact among the mass of fibers and hinders the shrinking process. Try to keep the solution hot by holding it in a hot-water bath, in a thermos, or by adding more hot water to the solution as you need it.

Additional Materials for Experimentation

You might like to have these on hand so you can try some exciting variations.

• a variety of yarns for decorating the felt beads, such as leftover knitting yarns of 80 to 100 percent wool, mohair, or novelty blends

• metallic, iridescent, or holographic fibers; dog hair; cotton or silk embroidery thread; glass seed beads

• objects to felt over, such as big buttons, triangular plastic buckles, and wooden macramé beads

• precious objects like ceramic fragments, costume jewels, shells, or stones to encase with felt

✖ **NOTE:** Remember to keep your wool and projects in plastic bags with a few mothballs; the same insects that dine on your nice sweaters may also find a way to enjoy your materials and beads for dessert.

Felting tools and materials (l to r): rough, woven cloth; shampoo and felting solutions, sushi mat, timer, spaghetti server, wool top, scissors

Tools

You'll find many of these items around the house. Don't return kitchen items to food service if they're used for dyeing.

Use a capped plastic bottle for the felting solution. Puncture small holes in the cap and use it as a shower-type dispenser. The felting solution is made from inexpensive shampoo that is colorless, odorless, and conditioner-free. You'll also need a bar of natural vegetable based soap without any color or fragrance additives, such as olive soap. Old towels, or old cotton or linen sheets, will help keep the bamboo or sushi mat from slipping around on your work surface as you roll the felt. If you don't have such a mat, try using some other slightly rough surface, such as a heavy canvas fabric. A large basin, bowl, or bucket will be needed, as well as a timer and some sharp scissors. A balance scale or digital kitchen scale (up to 18 ounces [500 g]), or a postage scale, will help you accurately weigh small amounts of wool, so that you'll be able to make beads of a consistent size.

A simple timer is used to keep track of your rolling time.

Finally, a spaghetti spoon, used to measure dry pasta into serving sizes, will help you obtain a consistent bead size.

Digital kitchen scale

Basic Techniques: Wool Magic

To begin your felt bead making experience, I recommend that you divide four colors of wool into premeasured weights, in order to practice making different sizes of beads. Each size requires a little more preparation time as well as an increase in the duration of rolling time. Making anything smaller than your fingers is difficult for anyone at first, so it's best to start big and reduce the amount of materials bit by bit.

The size and hardness of a felt bead depends in large part on how much wool you use and on the length of your rolling, or felting, time. The spaghetti serving-sizer (or a similar device) and a timer will help you get a bead of consistent size. Use a timer, also check the hardness of the bead by squeezing it with your fingers. Begin the rolling time once you have all the layers put together. As a starting point, I suggest that you make these practice beads, following these instructions on the next page.

EXTRA LARGE
1/3 ounce (11g) green wool made from 12 layers; minimum 10 minutes rolling

LARGE BEAD
1/4 ounce (8 g) blue wool made from nine layers; minimum 8 minutes rolling

MEDIUM BEAD
1/5 ounce (5 g) red wool made from six layers; minimum seven minutes rolling

SMALL BEAD
1/10 ounce (2 g) yellow wool, made from three layers; minimum five minutes rolling

Making Basic Beads, Pendants & Balls

Once you start working with wetted wool, it will take all your attention, so I suggest that you do all the preparation before wetting your hands and beginning the felting.

PHOTO 1

1. Weigh out your wool per bead, dividing it into several layers. If you're making a medium bead, for example, you'll make the wool layers by first roughly dividing the wool into four piles; set aside two of them. Now pull little tufts from one of the remaining sections, layering them one on top of each other in various directions, as shown in photo 1. Make two fluffy piles, and repeat this layering process for the other section. This will help the fibers blend easily during the felting process. Since the final outer layer of the bead will act like a veil, enclosing the other core fibers in a smooth and tight final layer, make one pile into a thinner layer.

2. Begin your bead by rolling up the first tuft of wool in a tight ball between your fingers; see photo 2. Wet it with hot felting solution. Wrap the next tuft in the opposite direction, as tightly as you can around this ball, to make the core of the bead; wet it completely.

3. Continue wrapping the remaining wool, layer by layer, around the core. It's important to roll each layer evenly, without any wrinkles on the surface. You needn't rewet it after adding an additional layer, but if you find that you're losing control of the material it's helpful to keep it in place by wetting the surface. As the bead gets larger you may find it easier to do the wrapping on the tabletop, using both hands to control the wool.

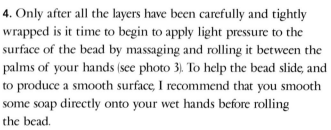
PHOTO 2

PHOTO 3

4. Only after all the layers have been carefully and tightly wrapped is it time to begin to apply light pressure to the surface of the bead by massaging and rolling it between the palms of your hands (see photo 3). To help the bead slide, and to produce a smooth surface, I recommend that you smooth some soap directly onto your wet hands before rolling the bead.

Start with very light pressure; as the air and excess felting solution escape, the fibers will begin to migrate and mass together, and the diameter of the bead will become smaller. After a few minutes, gradually increase the pressure. You'll find that the bead is shrinking in size but gaining in hardness. Periodically, squeeze the ball as hard as you can several times, forcing the fibers to turn toward the core (this is the direction in which you want the bead to shrink); wet it with felting solution and continuing rolling.

5. Check your watch, and time how long it takes you to make a hard, well-shaped bead. If your bead looks dry, or if little flaps of wool start sticking out from its surface, you can apply more hot felting solution as you roll the bead. (Some moisture will dissipate during the rolling, and a rise in temperature helps the fibers shrink during the final stages of the process.) Keep your hands well soaped, but not too slippery.

6. When you're happy with the size and hardness of your bead, rinse it well in hot water several times, and squeeze it dry in a clean towel. Reshape the bead, if necessary, and leave it to dry.

Variations on the Basic Bead

Simple variations are made by blending different materials into the outer layer of wool; they'll add color and texture to your felt beads.

- Blend a little metallic or holographic fiber to make glitter balls of colored wool.

- Marbleized effects are made by roughly blending complementary colors of wool between your fingers, or by crisscrossing narrow wisps of contrasting colors over each other

- Make fine lines by tightly winding wool yarn around the bead after the final color layer is wrapped and wetted

- Stitch seed beads onto the surface, or embroider images onto a dry bead

- Burn or cut into the surface of the dry bead, exposing the inner color(s); I used a soldering iron to create patterns and a craft knife to make carvings

- "Geodes" can be made by making beads of various color layers; after the bead is completed, cut it in half to expose its multicolored core

- Try mixing in unusual materials, such as peat, human hair, or wee bits of cut silk, linen, or cotton embroidery threads

- Make a bead from your pet's fur (I used English sheepdog), or mix some of it into the wool

- Encase your favorite object, such as a china fragment, a seashore treasure, or a favorite stone by felting a thick skin of wool all around it, then cutting an opening in the front to expose the object

- Shape the bead into a cube or oval with your fingers. At the final stages of shrinking the bead, while it's still slightly soft, compress and mold the bead for several minutes, until it retains the new shape on its own, then wash and squeeze it dry

Now you have the information that you need to go on to make great felt beads of all kinds!

Crescent Moon Pendant

Longer shaped beads are fun to make, but they present a real challenge when it comes time to stringing them together. A neat solution is to begin by creating the bead with its cord on the inside; after completion you can string smaller beads onto the cord.

JORIE JOHNSON

Making Beautiful **Beads**

MATERIALS & TOOLS

⅓ ounce (10 g) fine white merino top, for large crescent moon
Scissors
Bamboo or sushi mat
Old, lint-free fabric, such as a pillowcase or sheet
Small amounts of dyed merino wool for surface design, in several colors
Short lengths of assorted novelty yarns (check the wool content), for decoration
33 inches (1 m) linen cord with nylon core, 1⁄16 inch (2 mm) in diameter (see note, below)
Two small glass beads; optional

DESIGNER'S NOTE:
I recommend linen cord with nylon core because it is water-resistant.

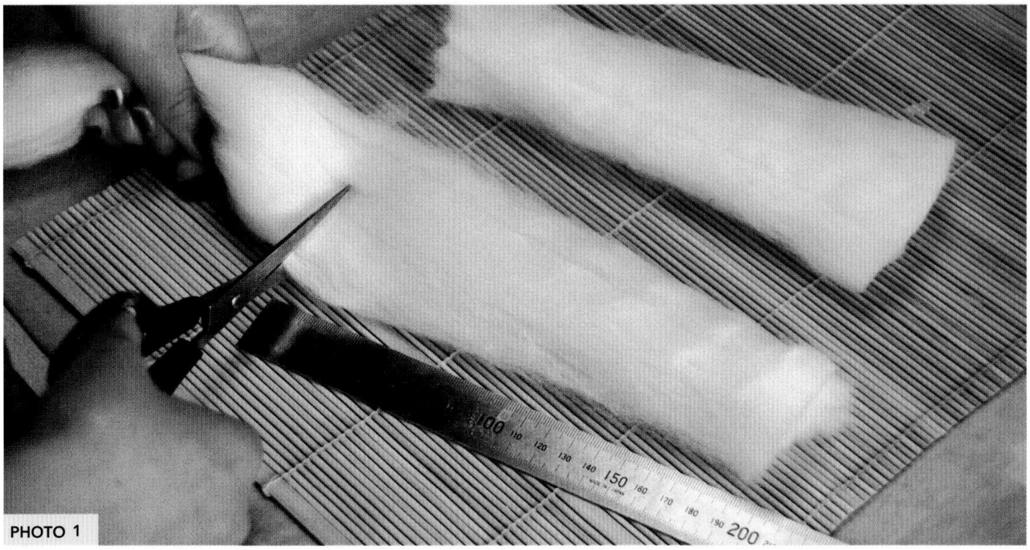

PHOTO 1

INSTRUCTIONS

1. To make the core, use scissors to cut two 8-inch (20 cm) lengths of white wool top, as shown in photo 1. Lay the bamboo mat on top of the old sheet (you may use a towel, but it's a nuisance if the loops of terry cloth fabric find their way into the mat during the rolling); moisten the mat with felting solution. Place one of the lengths of white top on the bamboo mat and spread it to approximately twice its original width. Sprinkle the wool with a little more felting solution. Find the center of the length of the cord, and place it near the edge of the wool (see photo 2), then roll them up tightly together, as shown in photo 3.

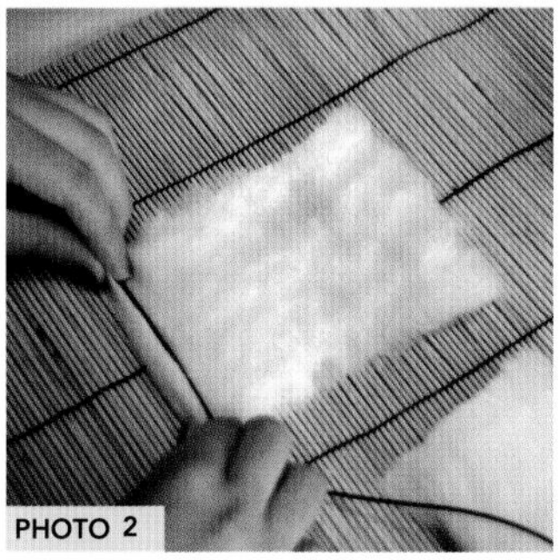
PHOTO 2

2. Roll 20 times in the mat (see photo 4). Next, place this roll at the edge of the second white wool length, which has also been spread out to twice its width, then moisten again, rolling them tightly together 20 times. This will be the core of the bead.

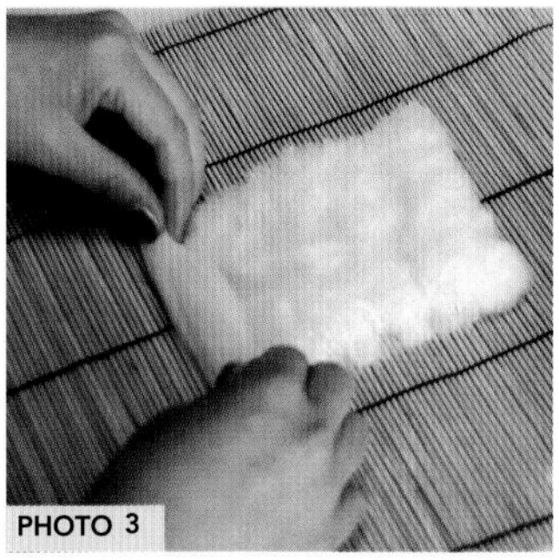
PHOTO 3

3. To make the decorative layers, visually divide the core into halves or thirds by wrapping two or three colors in several thin layers around the core, with each color slightly overlapping another, as shown in photos 5 and 6. It's fun to use bright, contrasting colors, or three colors that blend into each other, to create a beautiful gradation. Be careful that each of the layers is of equal thickness, and that no white areas of the core can be seen after you've rolled the bead another 20 times in the mat. This is the first of the design layers.

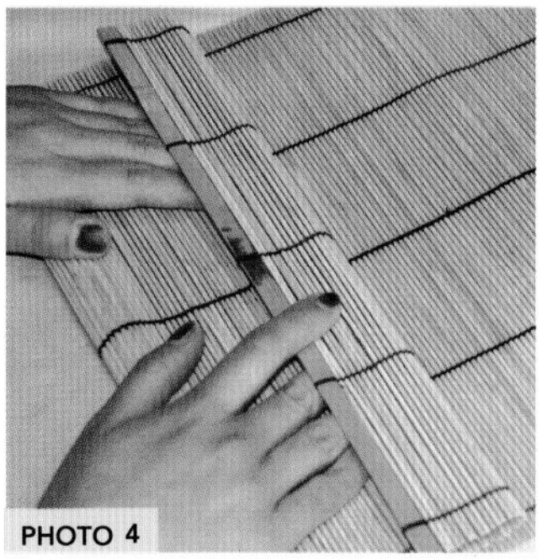
PHOTO 4

PHOTO 5

4. Before felting any further, wrap the final design layer around the bead. From the novelty yarns you have, choose several interesting colors and textures that will complement each other, and wrap short lengths of each one tightly around the core (see photo 7). With the tip of a scissor blade, slip the end of the yarn under a neighboring strand of yarn, to secure it. Experiment with different color schemes and various wrapping intervals to determine the best balance of design and color.

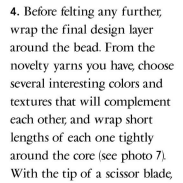

PHOTO 8

5. Roll 50 times in the bamboo mat (see photo 8). Place the bead in the palm of your hand and massage it in the lengthwise direction, rubbing the surface carefully back and forth about 50 times, as shown in photo 9, occasionally rotating the bead; both the mat rolling and hand rubbing are considered one set. Repeat four to five times, applying more hot felting solution or soap as needed, to help the surface fibers felt into the core wool.

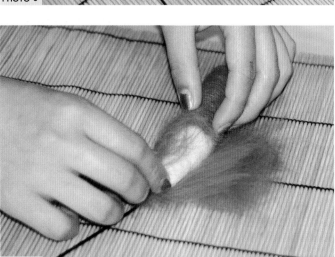

PHOTO 6

PHOTO 7

PHOTO 9

PHOTO 10

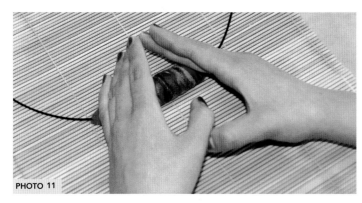

PHOTO 11

PHOTO 12

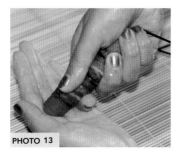

PHOTO 13

Some of the wool will tend to slip off the rounded core, toward each end of the bead, so force it back into position between stints of rolling (see photo 10). Be gentle at first, or the yarn will move about too much. Apply gentle pressure until it's obvious the yarns are adhering and staying in position.

6. In order to avoid elongating the shape, place your hands in a slanted position and, working from the outer edges toward the center of the bead, roll it on top of the mat (see photo 11); this way the wool will tend to gather toward the center of the bead. Try to form a good-looking crescent shape with a thick center and tapering ends. Roll and harden it until you've embedded all the outermost design yarns into the surface of the bead and it's as hard as a rubber ball.

7. Referring to photo 12, make a nice curved shape by holding both ends of the bead and the cord in your right hand, with the center curve of the bead resting in the palm of your left hand. Massage the arc with your left hand.

8. When you've achieved the desired shape, size, and firmness, rinse the bead well in hot water, and wring it in a clean towel. Reshape the bead, and leave it to dry.

9. Sometimes a bead looks hairy after it dries. This may be due to the quality of the wool you are using, the blend of fibers in the novelty yarn, or the rough surface of the mat. Using a pair of sharp scissors, trim excess hairs from the surface of the bead. (Now there's a new use for that sweater shaver your aunt gave you for Christmas some years ago. You'll find you can't live without one again! To remove any undesirable longer hairs, carefully "brush" the surface of the bead with the shaver.)

10. The bead is now ready to combine with other beads, or you can use it as it is. To disguise the cut ends of the cord, glue a small glass bead to each end, let dry, and then tie a knot in the cord so that it hangs at a suitable length. To make a smaller, more stout crescent moon bead, cut .28 ounces (8 g) of the white wool top into three 4-inch (10 cm) lengths, and proceed as described above. Roll this bead more often in your hands in the beginning stages, so that the ends stay rounded instead of tapering. Place the bead in the curve of your hand and massage it lengthwise. The wool has a tendency to spread out along the cord during the rolling, so try cinching both ends of the cord together, forcing the wool to gather toward the center of the bead. You should also slip one end of the cord between your index finger and middle finger and massage the end of the bead while twisting it into your tightly closed fingers (see photo 13); repeat again for the other end of the bead. Remember to work the bead in the direction or area you want it to be shaped.

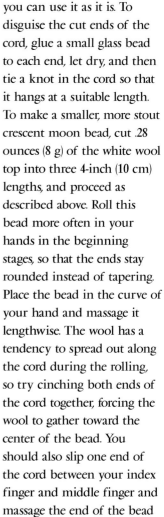

Felt beads in interesting shapes make fabulous, playful necklaces. You'll see how these woolen beads complement your winter wardrobe of soft mohair sweaters and woolen jackets. For this project, several items are used that allow a thick cord to pass through the bead. You can even make your own cord!

Unusually Shaped Felt Beads

JORIE JOHNSON

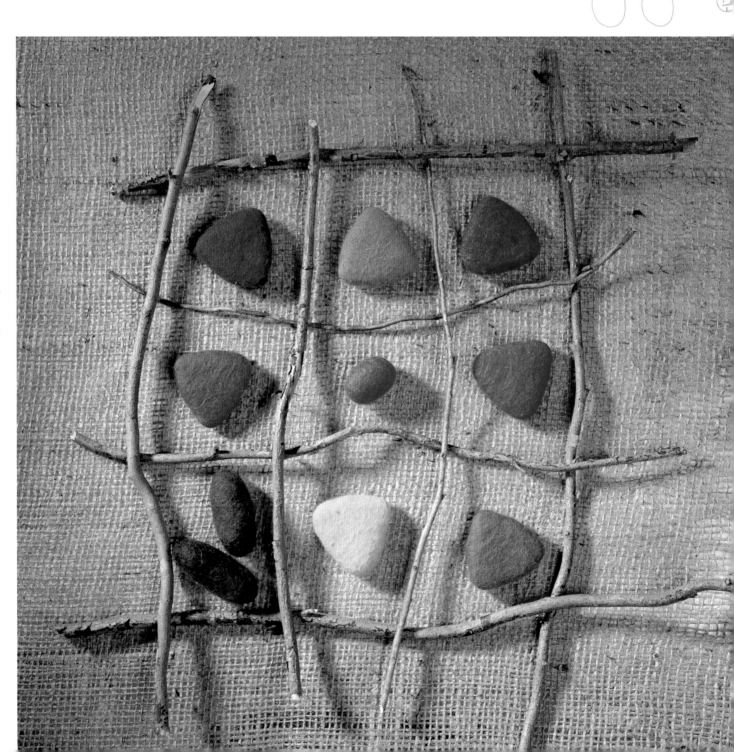

MATERIALS & TOOLS

Fine merino wool, in a variety of colors (quantity varies with size of object; see below)

Wooden macramé bead, ⅝ x ¾ inch (1.5 x 2 cm); .03 ounces (1g) wool in four layers; minimum five minutes of felting time

Wooden toggle button ⅝ x 1¾ inches (1.5 x 4.6 cm); ¹⁄₁₀ ounce (1.5 g) wool in four layers; minimum five minutes of felting time

Triangular plastic buckle 1½ inches (3.9 cm) on each side; ¹⁄₁₀ ounce (2 g) wool in five layers; minimum 10 minutes of felting time

Scale

Felting solution

Bar of soap

Basin

Timer

White craft glue; optional

Towel, for occasionally drying your hands

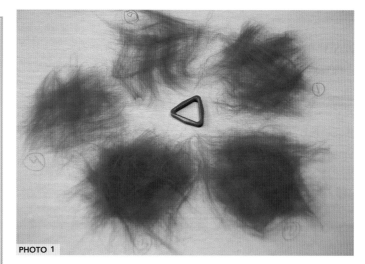

PHOTO 1

PHOTO 2

PHOTO 3

INSTRUCTIONS

✖ **DESIGNER'S NOTE:**

This is a variation on the basic bead making process. A well-felted bead becomes so dense that you must plan how you'll allow for a thick cord to pass through it. One way to make a hole in the center of the bead is by felting around a small object that has a large opening already in it, such as a wooden or plastic button or a macramé bead.

1. Divide the amount of wool required for an individual bead into several piles, each pile composed of several thin layers of wool laid in various directions on top of each other, as shown in photo 1. The outer layers should be the thinnest; they'll encase the object like a fine veil.

2. Carefully wrap the object up in the wool, layer by layer, as shown in photo 2, wetting with the felting solution when necessary and being careful that the overall shape is of even thickness. The wool will tend to slide off toward the edges of the buckle or macramé bead, so take care. Alternate the direction of the fibers when you're winding the layers of wool around the center core object.

3. Apply a little soap directly onto your hands, and start gently massaging the bead by rolling it in the palm of your hands. Because you're now working with an unusual shape, you may find the beginning felting stages more difficult. As the wool begins to tighten and shrink around the object, slowly apply more pressure. Continue felting for the minimum required amount of time, changing directions often, periodically squeezing the bead, and remembering to work the edges, too (see photo 3). It's up to you to control the shape and desired size. It's naturally more challenging to felt

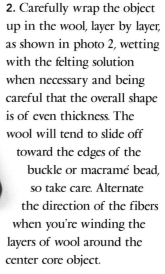

PHOTO 4

around a solid object than a more malleable, 100% wool bead, so keep at it until the outer fibers are well felted.

4. After completion, wash the beads well in hot water (see photo 4), squeeze out the excess liquid in a towel, and leave them to dry completely. If after inspecting the dry bead you feel it hasn't been felted enough, or the size isn't consistent, apply more hot felting solution and continue felting the bead until the desired size, shape, or hardness is achieved; then rinse it well, squeeze out the excess liquid in a clean towel, and let dry.

5. To further harden the outer surface of the bead, and to reduce the appearance of fur balls later on, I recommended that you apply a milliner's hat stiffener (used for winter hats) with a brush to the surface of the dry bead. A simpler method is

to apply diluted white craft glue while the bead is still damp. Use a brush, or roll the bead in a saucer that has a bit of glue diluted with water to the consistency of skim milk, then squeeze out the excess glue.

6. To pierce a dry bead with ease, pass a thick needle, such as an upholstery needle (which has a big eye for threading thick cords, leather thongs, and various ribbons) through the bead's hollow center. For shapes like the triangle, pierce the bead through a corner rather than stringing it through the center.

Thick Felt Cords for Your Special Beads

MATERIALS & TOOLS

33 inches (1 m)
merino wool top
Bamboo mat
Old cotton sheet
Felting solution
Bar of soap

1. In order to make a cord, you must first gauge how much wool you'll need before you actually separate it from the hank. Partially separate a narrow lengthwise section of the merino top from the cut length, in a manner similar to dividing hair into sections for braiding, as shown in photo 5; it should be approximately one-half the width of your index finger. Take the wool in your hands and twist a small section of its width (equal to approximately $1/6$ or $1/8$ of its diameter) between your fingers (see photo 6). This helps you to roughly establish the cord's final diameter. Don't twist it more than one and a half times, because it's not possible to

PHOTO 5

PHOTO 6

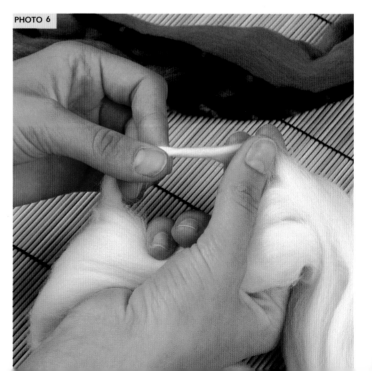

make a felt cord that dense. If the slightly twisted area appears too thin, try twisting a wider section. If it's too thick, release some of the wool and try sample-twisting a smaller section. Only when you've succeeded in finding the appropriate diameter of the cord for your project should you separate the entire length of wool from the rest of the top by carefully pulling it away hand width by hand width, down the entire 33-inch (1 m) length.

2. Check the separated top for any areas that are slightly fatter than others. It's difficult to remove bits of wool from the thicker areas, but it's easy to thin these areas by pulling ever so slightly at the soft rope, in the lengthwise direction thereby reducing the quantity of fibers in that area.

3. Place the bamboo mat on the sheet. This will not only keep the mat from slipping during the rolling process, but also absorb any excess liquid. Moisten the mat with a little felting solution; lay down the soft wool top and sprinkle a little solution over the section lying on the mat. Roll with the fingertips 10 times on top of the mat, shifting section by section onto the mat, until the entire length of the wool top becomes a rounder cordlike form.

4. As the cord begins to take form, sprinkle it with more felting solution and roll it inside the mat, 10 times per section. After you've felted the entire cord once, apply more pressure for each new sequence, increasing to 20 rolls per section, until the cord is strong enough to tow your car!

You'll be amazed when you see that the cord can shrink up to 20 percent, so take care to start with a sufficient length. To check if the cord has shrunk enough, try separating it widthwise between your fingernails. Does it separate easily? If it does, this is a sign to keep rolling until it's *impossible* to spread it apart.

Cord Variations

Before felting, twist two colors of thin merino wool top lengths together to create a striking two-tone cord. Or felt shorter sections of colors together to create multicolored ropes. It's difficult to felt two wet ends together, so overlap the areas of color you wish to join while the wool is still dry, then sprinkle a little felting solution over the wool and roll it carefully with the pressure from your fingers on top of the bamboo mat (or any other slightly rough surface, such as a heavy canvas fabric). The most difficult areas are joints where the ends of two sections overlap, so take time to evenly distribute the wool so that the cord will be the same thickness from end to end.

A felt cord can really complement your work because you can coordinate its color and thickness as desired. Wouldn't you agree that a unique bead or pendant deserves a unique cord?

Shibori Resist Dyed Beads

This fun and whimsical bead is transformed with an easy overdye. Make some new beads in bright colors, or use some from the leftover not-so-nice collection you may have, and experiment with overdyeing them to achieve an interesting resist pattern and a unique shape. You must overdye in a shade that's darker than the color of the bead. Here, I dyed a variety of bright merino felt beads in ebony black.

JORIE JOHNSON

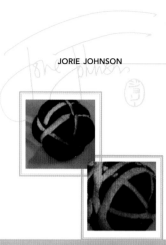

MATERIALS & TOOLS

18 to 20 felt beads, each made from ¼ ounce (8 g) fine merino wool

Assortment of wide, thick, and small rubber bands

Plastic net, used for potato or onion bags

6-quart (6 L) stainless or unchipped enamel pot

Mixing cup and old stainless steel spoon for mixing dye

Measuring teaspoon

Acid wool dye, in a shade darker than the beads*

Table salt*

Large stainless steel spoon or stirring rod

Newspapers

Dye thermometer; optional

Rubber gloves

Timer

* Living in Japan, I use Dylon Multipurpose Craft Dye, Ebony #8 (www.dylon.co.uk), which is available almost everywhere except the USA. This dye is actually a *combination* of dye types, including the acid dye formulation necessary for dyeing wool. You must add salt to it in order to get results similar to mine. In the USA, I recommend that you use any type of hot-water dye that is suitable for wool, to which you will have to add a weak acid, such as distilled vinegar. Follow the manufacturer's instructions, but you'll probably need to experiment a bit, too. To get a rich black, you'll use more dye powder (up to a maximum of 6 percent of the weight of the wool you're dyeing) than with other colors, but you'll probably be able to dye more than this quantity, because the dye penetrates only a thin layer of the dense felt material.

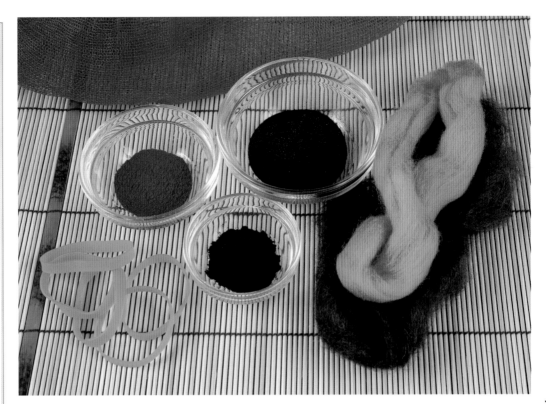

INSTRUCTIONS

✖ **DESIGNER'S NOTE:** Can you imagine how I got this unusual shape? The answer is in the rubber band that was tightly wound around the bead. During the dyeing process, the tension of the rubber band keeps the dye from penetrating the surface. The result is a distinct line of the original color; simultaneously, the round shape becomes distorted in the hot dye bath. If you'd like to use smaller beads, use the same amount of wool to make more beads, in different weights and sizes, for the same amount of dye. With the shibori resist dye technique, the more you wrap the surface of the bead, the larger the area of original color remains after dyeing. You'll soon get inquisitve comments about your creations, but go ahead and keep our secret!

1. Make 20 or so large, colorful felt beads, keeping them slightly soft, as described on pages 11—12.

2. While the beads are still damp, tightly wrap a rubber band around each one, distributing the pressure evenly around the surface. To help spread out the wrapped areas, use the tine of a fork to untwist, lift, and separate the rubber band in crowded areas. After the rubber band is well positioned on the bead, further compress the beads by squashing them between your fingers, in order to deepen the creases around the rubber band.

It's easier for the rubber band to grab the surface of a slightly soft bead and to create a bit of an indentation, recessing the edge of the rubber band into the surface of the bead, and thus ensuring a better resist during the dyeing process. Experiment with rubber bands of various widths and lengths, depending on the size of the bead you make.

3. The felt beads should be thoroughly wetted in a bath of warm water (with a few drops of dishwashing liquid) before dyeing them. The dye will be absorbed more evenly if the beads are presoaked, or if they're dyed directly after felting, while still wet. Place the beads in a plastic net (make sure the net is made from a material that is least likely to absorb much of the

PHOTO 1

dye itself). The net will make it easier to fish the beads out of the dye bath at any point in order to check the depth and suitability of the color; it will also help you to keep the beads submerged in the dye bath.

4. Follow the directions on the package of dye that you purchased. (For Dylon dye, I placed one .2-ounce [5.6 g] container of the wool dye, in Ebony Black #8, plus 1 level teaspoon [5 g] of salt in a mixing cup such as an old coffee cup, and diluted them with a good amount of boiling water.) Take precautions and mix the dye and salt solution over several sheets of old newspaper, as the dye

is extremely concentrated and can stain the surface of anything it drips onto, including your own hands. As a health precaution, never use dyeing equipment, such as pots or stirrers, for food preparation, and be sure to wear rubber gloves.

5. Fill the dye pot halfway with 90 ounces (3000 cc) of water. As the temperature starts to rise, add the dye/salt solution; stir, then slowly lower the net, with the beads inside it, into the dye pot. Bring the temperature up to just below the boiling point (205° F, or 96° C).

6. Keep the temperature high and continue cooking

for 30 minutes, stirring occasionally and making sure the beads are below the surface of the dye bath at all times. This ensures a consistent color throughout the surface of the beads.

7. After the allotted time, turn off the heat and allow the dye bath to cool. If you're in a hurry, you may rinse the beads immediately, but more of the dye may be absorbed during the cooling process.

8. Remove the beads from the cooled dye bath, and rinse them well while squeezing them under hot running water. Continue rinsing until the water runs

clear, then twist the beads in a towel to wring out the excess moisture.

There will be little color remaining in the pot after your dyeing session is over. If the liquid from an all-acid-base dye is visibly clear at this point, it means the dye has been completely absorbed into the goods and the remaining ingredients—water and salt—are safe to discard in the environment; otherwise, follow the manufacturer's directions for disposal. If there is a lot of color left, it's possible to use the remaining dye bath for a second, lighter dyeing round. If you have some other felt samples you want to experiment with, or a bit of silk fabric or silk ribbon that you'd like to dye, this is the perfect opportunity to blot up the remaining dye. Maybe you could tie-dye some exciting felt cords with this extra color.

9. Remove the rubber bands from around the beads (see photo 1), and leave them to dry.

Barrel Bead Necklace by Joi Rae; loose beads, 1998.
Wool, silk/wool novelty yarns, wooden beads; bead size:
2.4 cm (w) x 3 cm (l). Photo by K. Nishimura;
Ikat table runner by J. Tomita

JORIE JOHNSON

Living at the end of the Silk Road to the East, as I have for the past 12 years, has really aided in the development of my textile horizons. Japan is not intrinsically a wool country but rather one of silk and bast fibers, yet the interest in my work and teaching has been well received because of the nature of the "newer" material and the experimental crossing of the threshold into a contemporary field of feltmaking—not for survival, but for pure pleasure and indulgence.

Frequently I exhibit in Japan, as well as internationally, and have works acquired by the Bank of Boston, the Victoria & Albert museum, and in many private collec-

tions. I recently received an award from the Japanese Textile Designers Association. I've accepted short-term lecturing positions in the USA and Japan, including Haystack School Of Arts and Crafts, Rhode Island School of Design Summer Textile Institute, Kyoto University of Art and Design, and Tama University of Art, as well asprivate workshops and international felt symposia throughout Europe. I have joined several research expeditions to central and eastern Asia, including Georgia, Mongolia, Kazakhstan, and Kyrgyzstan. I've been a contributing artist to books such as *Fiberarts Design Books 2* and *6, Fiberarts* magazine, *Surface Design* magazine, and other international textile publications.

Barrel Bead Necklace II by Joi Rae, 1998. Wool, silk/wool novelty yarns, wooden beads; bead size: 2.4 cm (w) x 3 cm (l). Photo by K. Nishimura; braided felt muffler by J. Johnson

Please visit my home page for more information (www.amsinet.ne.jp/~joirae/).

With all the constant and mad running around that a typical urban person does these days, I know why the herders of central Asia were called no-mad-ic. I respect and praise the peoples of history, past and present, who had no choice other than to make their homes of felt and, further, highly respected the animal from which their sustenance was ensured.

Felt GALLERY

Hand Rolled Felt Beads, Victoria Brown, 1999. ¾ in. (1.9 cm). Photo by artist

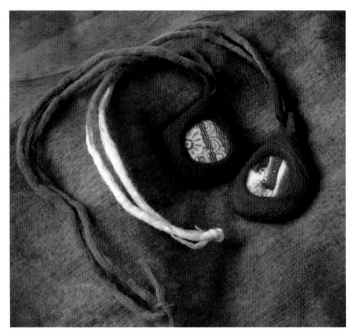

Drifter Series: *China Fragments*, Yumiko Yanagihara, 2001.
Left: 2¾ x 2¼ x ⅜ in. (7 x 6 x 1 cm); right: 3¼ x 2 x ⅜ in.
(8 x 5 x 1 cm). Photo by Evan Bracken

Multi-Colored Bead Necklace,
Jean Hicks, 2001. Small: ¾ in.
(2 cm); large: 1½ in. (3.8 cm).
Photo by Evan Bracken

Collier of Felt Beads, Gerda Kohlmayr, 2000. 1¼ in. (3 cm). Photo by artist

Drifter Series: Thai Buddha, Yumiko Yanagihara, 2001. 2 x 1¼ x ⅜ in. (5 x 3 x 1 cm). Photo by Evan Bracken

Remembers, Leena Sipilä, 2001. Recycled handmade felt clothing fabric; bead size: 1 cm diameter x 1 cm. thickness. Photo by L. Vossi

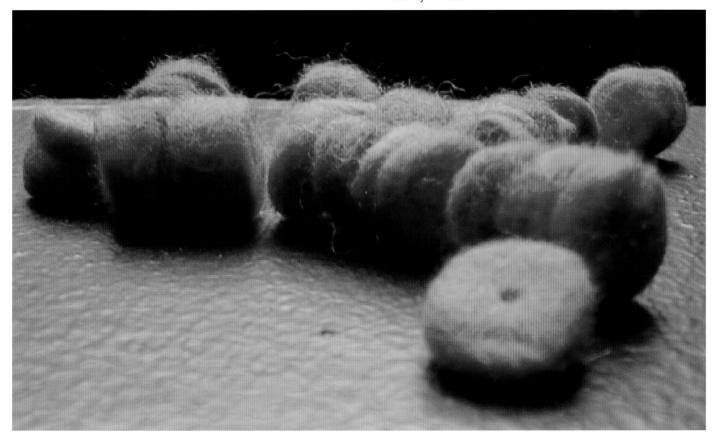

Introduction to Paper

BY ANN MARIE KENNEDY

Sheet pulp (top and left); cotton linter

Paper is a fascinating material with a long history. When paper is made from the cellulose found in plant fibers, it's a very malleable material to work with and holds many creative possibilities. In Asia, sculptural paper has long had many practical uses, such as for umbrellas and clothing. There are wide differences in the quality and strength of handmade paper (made from cotton, flax, or abaca) as compared with commercially made paper, which is made from nonrenewable wood pulp. You'll find that making beads from natural fiber paper is an accessible, low-tech medium; there are no specialized tools or equipment needed to begin, and it's even non-toxic. In this section, we'll explore two methods for making beads from paper.

Basics

Paper beads can be made using either sculptural papermaking techniques or papier maché. Adding natural plant materials taken from your own surroundings makes handmade paper even more special.

Starting with Fiber

Bead making with paper pulp requires basic kitchen tools. You'll need a dedicated (nonfood) blender, plastic containers, a colander or finely woven material (such as mosquito netting, muslin, or even interfacing) for straining, and a work space that can withstand moisture. Paper pulp can be made at home or purchased in a prepared state from a supplier who specializes in hand papermaking supplies. Paper pulp is made from macerated, or softened, fiber and water. You can start with the basic *sheet pulp*, which is raw fiber that has been pulped at a papermill, then dried into sheets. The sheet pulp is then mixed in a blender with an additive to make a workable pulp.

Papermaking tools and materials (l to r): skewers, straightedge, blender, whisk, colander, mosquito netting, methylcellulose, assorted pigments, digital kitchen scale

There are several additives that are used to bind the pulp together before it's ready to be sculpted into a bead shape you want. Once dry, the finished piece can then be left in its natural condition, or decorated. Papier-maché is a process that uses ready-made or recycled paper and some kind of paste, commonly wallpaper paste. You can get some nice effects if you use handmade paper, which is available in beautiful colors and may have been made with interesting plant materials, flower petals, or even metallic threads or flakes. The paper is first torn or cut into small pieces and soaked in the paste. Then the pieces of paper are laid over a sub-structure, like a crumpled ball of paper, a wooden bead, or even a paper pulp bead. Continue to add pieces of paper until the surface is built up to $^1/_8$ inch (3 mm) thick. Finally, the papier-maché is left to dry completely, then finished with paints or other decorative treatments.

Making Pulp

For bead making or any sculptural process, a type of short-fiber, low-shrinkage sheet pulp called *cotton linter* is a good material to use. If you have a choice when purchasing it, ask for *first cut-grade* cotton linter.

Weigh the sheet pulp on a scale in 1-ounce (28 g) increments. Tear the sheet into small pieces, 1 x 1 inch (2.5 x 2.5 cm) or less, then put them into a blender with 16 ounces (.48 L) of water. Don't overload the blender, or you'll burn out the motor. If your water source is full of iron or other minerals, use distilled or filtered water or these particles could end up in the final piece. If you can't find a source of sheet pulp, recycled paper is another possibility. Try to stick with high-quality paper, office paper without ink, or scraps of art paper. Using the same measurements as above, first tear the paper into small pieces, cover with warm water, and soak overnight. This helps remove the sizing and other additives. Then rinse the paper well before hydrating it in a blender. There are many indigenous and garden plants that can be used in papermaking, too. The plant fiber can be added to pulp as a decorative element, or it can constitute the pulp material entirely.

Consult your library or local bookstore for books on the subject of hand papermaking for information on how to process plant fibers. Once you've hydrated the pulp, strain it in a colander lined with mosquito netting or a fine cloth to filter out the excess water.

Making Beautiful Beads

29

ADDITIVES

You have a choice of several additives to help the pulp hold the bead shape; they serve to bind the pulp together and fill the surface so that it will be smoother.

• Wallpaper paste, also known as methylcellulose, is a water-soluble powdered adhesive that comes in many grades. The best type to use for bead-making purposes is an archival grade of pure methylcellulose, available from art supply stores. Wallpaper paste that is available from hardware stores will work equally well, but it may yellow over time because of other, unknown chemical additives in it. To make a methylcellulose paste, slowly add 8 teaspoons (40 mL) of the powder to 4 ounces (118 mL) of boiling water. When the particles are dissolved, add 8 ounces (237 mL) of cold water. Stir until the mixture is smooth, then let the liquid cool for one hour.

• You may substitute white glue or matte medium for methylcellulose, but any time you substitute other additives, you'll need to experiment with them in order to get the proportions of all the ingredients right.

• Titanium dioxide pigment is another powdered additive that helps to create a smoother surface and adds opacity; it's available from a hand papermaking supplier.

• You can also substitute gesso, which is used to prime a canvas before painting, if you can't find titanium dioxide.

• Stand oil is a special form of thickened linseed oil you can use to add sheen and create a denser surface on the bead.

Techniques

Paper pulp needs to be the right consistency to be formed into a bead; if it's too runny, it will be difficult to shape. Once the pulp is strained and the additives are mixed in, test its consistency by rolling a small amount (use 1 teaspoon [5 g] for a ¾-inch [1.9 cm] bead) in the palms of your hands. If it doesn't form into a ball, there's too much water in the mixture. Strain the water by squeezing it in some cloth or mosquito netting. If you need to remove more water, let the mixture sit out for 24 hours. Enough water should evaporate to make the mixture workable.

Use water-soluble pigments to create rich, vibrant tones in paper pulp. It's best to use the highly saturated pigments, along with a retention aid, for this job; the ones available from a papermaking supplier are especially designed for paper pulp. Add small amounts of pigment to pulp in the blender, mixing after each addition, until a shade several shades darker or brighter than the desired shade is reached. Add the retention aid and mix with the pulp. Let the mixture rest for 15 minutes. If you can't get these specialized pigments, you can paint the bead with water-soluble paints when it's dry.

Round beads can be made by rolling the pulp mixture in the palms of your hands or with the palm of one hand on a smooth surface, like a countertop. Roll the mixture back and forth to make a cylindrical shape, or form it with your fingers to make squares or organic shapes. Use the tips of your fingers to gently smooth the surface of the bead. Look for cracks and rough spots; they can be smoothed out or filled with small amounts of pulp.

Drying

Use a wire cookie rack to dry the finished beads. Find a warm, dry spot and leave the beads to dry. It may take up to 48 hours, depending on the environment. Drying them too close to a heat source, or with direct heat, may warp or shrink the beads. If you're in a hurry, let them dry overnight, then use a hair dryer set on low heat.

Be sure to bring a sense of adventure and experimentation to your bead-making sessions. Now that you have the basic material you need to create intriguing paper beads from pulp or papier-maché, you're ready to try some of these designs yourself.

Metallic Discs

The gleam of metal in a sculptured paper pulp makes these disc-shaped beads most unusual.

ANN MARIE KENNEDY

Making Beautiful **Beads**

MATERIALS & TOOLS

Cotton linter

Colander or strainer

Mosquito netting, sheer curtain material, or other fine mesh or cloth

Methylcellulose paste

Gesso

Titanium dioxide

Stand oil or linseed oil

Blender

Plastic containers, 1-quart (.95 L) size, and several small containers for water and mixing

Household object, such as a napkin ring or cookie cutter

Small copper beads with large holes

Gouache, acrylic, or tempera paints

Bronze powder or metallic ink

Paintbrushes

Acrylic varnish or spray fixative

PHOTO 1

PHOTO 2

DETAIL

INSTRUCTIONS

1. Mix 1 ounce (28 g) of cotton pulp to 16 ounces (480 mL) of water in the blender for one to two minutes.

2. Strain the mixture in a strainer lined with a fine cloth or netting, as shown in photo 1, or let it drain overnight.

3. Transfer the pulp into a plastic container or bowl, then add 3 teaspoons (15 mL) of methylcellulose paste, $^{1}/_{2}$ teaspoon (2.5 mL) of gesso, 2 teaspoons (10 mL) of titanium dioxide, and $^{3}/_{4}$ teaspoon (3.75 mL) of stand oil or linseed oil. If you don't have titanium dioxide, increase the amount of gesso to 3 teaspoons (15 mL), and strain the mixture. Mix well with a spoon or stirrer.

The mixture should be somewhat tacky and slightly dry, and have the consistency of bread dough. If it's runny, add more titanium dioxide. If it's still runny, strain the mixture with mesh, or let it stand overnight. Store the pulp mixture in the refrigerator if you won't be working with it in the next few days.

4. To form beads, flatten a small amount of pulp mixture (about 1 rounded teaspoon [5 mL]) between both hands to make a disc-shaped bead about $^{3}/_{4}$ inch (1.9 cm) wide, or use a small household object to create clean-edged shapes (see photo 2). To make square, flat beads, push the pulp into any suitably shaped object. For circle-shaped beads, press the pulp into a napkin ring or cookie cutter. The edges can be left thick, or squeezed to form thin edges. You can vary the amount for thicker or thinner beads, but try to keep track of the initial amount so you can maintain a consistent size.

PHOTO 3

5. Push a metal bead into the center of the disc, as shown in photo 3, and place small amounts of pulp around it to hold it in. Let the bead dry (see the drying instructions on page 31).

6. When the beads are completely dry, they can be painted. First, paint the beads with a layer of gesso. Then, mix a small amount of gouache paint with gesso to the desired shade; paint the bead and let it dry. Mix bronze powder with water and paint a light coat of this mixture on the bead (see photo 4). If you don't have bronze powder, use a thinned metallic ink (available from an art supply store). Let dry. Add another coat of the gouache/gesso mixture, and blot it with a paper towel.

Repeat these steps until the desired surface is achieved. The metallic pigment will fill the crevices and show through the coat of paint.

7. Finish each bead with two coats of acrylic varnish or a spray fixative.

PHOTO 4

Oversized Plaster Beads

Think of this bead as a tiny spherical canvas to which you can apply any kind of decorative paint treatment!

ANN MARIE KENNEDY

MATERIALS & TOOLS

Cotton linter

Plaster of Paris

Blender

Plastic containers, 1-quart (.95 L) size, and several small containers, for water and mixing

Gouache, acrylic, or tempera paint

Fine sandpaper, 400-grit or finer

Bamboo skewer

Metallic ink or pen

Paintbrush

Spray fixative

Spackle, optional

INSTRUCTIONS

✖ **DESIGNER'S NOTE:** It's important to not let any of the plaster liquid down the drain, as it could cause a clog. Instead, let the liquid drain into a container, let it harden, and then scrape it into the trash.

1. Mix 1 ounce (28 g) of cotton pulp to 16 ounces (480 mL) of water in the blender for one to two minutes.

2. Put 3 heaping teaspoons (15 g) of pulp into a plastic container. Add 4 ounces (112 g) of plaster, stirring until the consistency is similar to oatmeal.

PHOTO 1

PHOTO 2

Once the plaster is added, you'll need to work quickly, because it hardens within a few minutes. This short working time is the reason you'll have to mix small batches.

3. Squeeze the excess liquid from 1 teaspoon (5 mL) of wet pulp into a separate container. Form it into round or oval beads by rolling it between the palms of your hands (see photo 1).

4. To create a hole for the cord or string, gently twist a bamboo skewer through the center of the bead before it hardens, as shown in photo 2.

5. Rest the wet beads on skewers over the edges of a container, so the bead doesn't touch any surface while it dries. Let the bead dry completely (usually overnight), until the bead no longer feels cool to the touch.

PHOTO 3

6. When dry, fill in any irregularities or cracks with spackle. Let dry, then sand the surface of the bead with a very fine sandpaper (400-grit or finer) for a smooth surface.

7. Paint the bead with several coats of gesso. Let it dry between each coat, and lightly sand the surface before applying the next coat. The bead is now ready to be painted with water-soluble paints, as shown in photo 3, or you might try using a metallic ink or ink pen. The surface is quite absorbent and easy to paint or draw on.

8. Seal the surface with a spray fixative.

Rice Papier-Maché

Wooden beads covered with a papier-maché technique take on a new elegance when you use beautiful Asian rice papers.

ANN MARIE KENNEDY

MATERIALS & TOOLS

Rice paper

Methylcellulose paste

Several plastic containers or bowls, 1-quart (.95 L) size or smaller

Wooden bead or pulp bead

Paintbrush

Metal ruler

Craft knife

Acrylic varnish

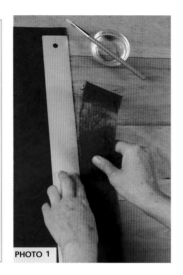

PHOTO 1

PHOTO 2

PHOTO 3

INSTRUCTIONS

✖ **DESIGNER'S NOTE:** For this project, I chose several types of decorative rice papers. These papers are thin and strong, and often have fibers or bits of bark running through them. Some common fibers they are made from are gampi, salago, mitsumata, lotka, or (perhaps more readily available) kozo, also called mulberry.

1. Tear the paper into long strips, ³/₈ inch (9 mm) wide. If the paper is difficult to tear, brush on a line of water along its length, and then tear the paper along that line, against the ruler, as shown in photo 1.

2. Tear these long strips into ¹/₂-inch (3.8 cm) pieces. It's important to tear rather than to cut the strips, because the fibrous edges made by tearing will help the strips bind smoothly together once they're on the bead.

3. Mix up some methylcellulose paste, as described on page 30, then thin it with water.

4. You need a support, such as a wooden craft or macramé bead, to paste the papers onto. (You can use a solid wood ball instead, if you drill a hole, ¹/₄ inch (6 mm) in diameter, through it.) If you use a wooden bead, you'll be able to cut the paper away from it after it's dry. Another option is to make some pulp beads, according to the instructions on page 33; these can be left in the final piece. For either type of support, choose a bead that is slightly smaller than the desired size.

Wet your fingers with some of the paste, and rub it on both sides of a small piece of dry paper (see photo 2). Lay this over the bead structure. Keep adding pieces of paste-covered paper, layering the pieces crosswise to each other, until four or five layers are built up. You may want to collage different colors or types of papers to the final layers for a decorative effect.

5. To smooth the surface, roll the bead between the palms of your hands. Let it dry completely.

6. Finish and seal the surface of the bead with an acrylic varnish (see photo 3).

I continue to use handmade paper in my sculptural and installation work, which has been exhibited both locally and nationally, and is in several collections. Recent awards include a New Works Grant from the North Carolina Art Council, and a three-month residency at Headlands Center for the Arts in California. I currently live in western North Carolina, where I am a resident artist at Penland School of Crafts.

Sprouted House, 1999. Cast paper with sprouted flax; 12 x 8 x 10 in. (30.5 x 20.3 x 25.4 cm). Photo by Tom Mills

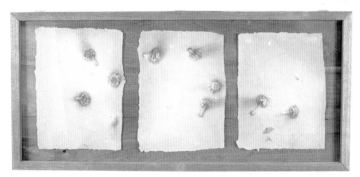

Clover, 1996. Flax paper and plants; 15 x 32 in. (38.1 x 81.2 cm). Photo by David Trawick

ANN MARIE KENNEDY

O ver the past 10 years much of my artwork has been influenced by my interest in hand papermaking. I began making paper in the basement of my parent's house, primarily experimenting with local plant fibers. Since then, my interests have branched into both traditional hand papermaking and using pulp as a material to create artwork. In 1998, I received the Master of Fine Arts in Intermedia and Sculpture at the University of Iowa. While there, I was employed at the University of Iowa Center for the Book Papermaking Facility as a research assistant in production papermaking.

From the Garden series, 1997. Flax paper and flowers; 19 x 25 in. (48.3 x 63.5 cm). Photo by David Trawick

Introduction to Polymer Clay

BY IRENE SEMANCHUK DEAN

Compared with other media, polymer clay is a mere infant in the art and craft world. Polymer clay was developed in the mid-twentieth century in Europe as a dollmaking medium, and within a couple of decades, it fell into the hands of a few artists. These artists recognized that its relative ease of use and incredible versatility make polymer clay an ideal medium for bead making.

Polymer clay isn't the same animal as the earthen clay that potters use. Polymer clay is made of PVC (polyvinyl chloride), mixed with plasticizers and color pigment. It's hardened by baking in a regular oven and doesn't change color or size when it's baked. Lightweight and colorfast, polymer clay is readily available at craft stores in small 2-ounce (56 g)—or slightly larger—packages, and it can be manipulated with simple methods as well as with complex techniques. Small wonder it's become so popular in such a short time!

Polymer clay comes in large and small blocks.

The Basics

Here's useful information that you should know about the basic characteristics and handling of polymer clay.

Using Polymer Clay

There are several brands of polymer clay available. The most important differences between them are in their prebaking malleability and in the strength and flexibility of finished pieces. Experiment with several brands to decide which is right for you.

Each brand offers upwards of 30 colors from which to choose—a rainbow feast for the eyes! You can also custom-blend colors to achieve your own personal shades; simply mix one or more colors together completely to create a new color.

CONDITIONING
All polymer clays, no matter how malleable they are right out of the package, must be conditioned. Conditioning thoroughly mixes the components and makes for a stronger finished piece. To condition by hand, start with 1 ounce (28 g) of clay. Warm it and squeeze it in your hands. Roll it into a long snake, fold it back onto itself, then roll it out again. Repeat this until the polymer stretches (instead of breaks) when you pull it apart. Try not to incorporate air bub-

Left to right: Acrylic rod, acrylic brayer, clay extruder and templates, pasta machine, and ceramic tile.

bles into the polymer as you condition it.

If you're willing to sacrifice that pasta machine you're not using anyway, you'll find it handy for working with polymer clay, especially when you're conditioning it. Cut the block of polymer into slabs just slightly thicker than the thickest setting on your pasta machine. Run a slab through the machine, fold it in half, and pass it through the machine again. Repeat this 15 to 20 times to thoroughly condition the polymer clay. Never feed the polymer into the rollers of the pasta machine with the fold on the top side; this will trap air bubbles in it. Conditioning is the perfect time to mix those new shades you've been planning to create.

If, after conditioning it, the polymer clay is too squishy, allow it to rest before working with it again. You won't need to recondition it unless it sits for several months.

BAKING

While polymer clay is a forgiving medium in many ways, it's very particular about its baking temperature. If the temperature is too low, the polymer will not completely fuse and the finished piece may be easily broken. If the temperature is too high, the polymer may burn and release noxious fumes. Most brands bake at 275° F (135° C); check the package of the brand you buy to make certain. I consider oven thermometers a necessity; they're widely available and very inexpensive.

You may want to follow my rules of thumb, as well as the package directions, about the clay's thickness and the length of baking time.

I bake for a minimum of 30 minutes, no matter how small or thin the piece, and up to an hour for larger, thicker pieces. If a piece isn't baked long enough, the polymer may not have a chance to fuse completely, and the finished piece may be weak. Baking for a longer time does no harm, as long as the temperature remains where it should.

CLEANUP & SAFETY

Polymer clay is certified nontoxic, but there are still some commonsense precautions. If you use kitchen tools for polymer clay, they shouldn't be used for food again. This means you'll have to dedicate that wedding-present pasta machine permanently to polymer clay, but you've probably made homemade pasta only once and it was a pain in the neck anyway. Objects that will come in contact with food shouldn't be made from polymer clay, nor should ashtrays or incense burners.

Polymer clay leaves a residue on your hands while you work with it. Many people clean up with alcohol-based baby wipes, but my preference is hand lotion. The lotion seems to break down the polymer clay, and I rub it off with a rough terrycloth rag. After that, I scrub with soap and a nail brush to remove all traces from my knuckles and fingernails.

Bake your beads on standing T-pins.

Don't breathe polymer fumes while baking, and use an exhaust fan as a precaution. A dedicated oven is ideal, but not always practical. Continued use of any oven for polymer clay will coat the inside oven walls with an oily film. Either wipe the oven down after baking polymer (I prefer to use baking soda and water as a mildly abrasive cleaner), or bake in a dedicated covered roasting pan. You can also cover your baking tray with aluminum foil. In the meantime, if you think you'll be pursuing polymer clay as a hobby, scout out yard sales or resale shops for a used toaster oven. Be sure to get an oven thermometer to ensure you're baking the clay at the right temperature.

STORAGE

Keep your polymer clay away from heat and direct sunlight. Store it in plastic food bags or plastic lidded containers. Polymer reacts with some plastics, so be sure to wrap it in waxed paper first.

Polymer clay is a magnet for dust, pet hair, and chenille sweater fuzz! Put it away when you're not using it. Polymer clay will retain its workability almost indefinitely if properly stored. You may need to recondition it after a period of time, but all of its working properties will be intact.

Tools

As mentioned above, a pasta machine makes quick work of conditioning polymer clay. It's also perfect for rolling uniformly thin sheets of polymer for various projects. Acceptable substitutes for a pasta machine are a printer's brayer or an acrylic rod. These won't help with conditioning, of course, but you can use them to roll polymer clay into sheets. Avoid wooden rolling tools, as these aren't able to roll a perfectly smooth surface and they're difficult to clean. To achieve a sheet of uniform thickness, use the brayer or other roller between two same-size objects, such as dowels or skewers (see photo 1).

A clay gun is a handy tool for extruding lengths of polymer clay. It's very similar to a cookie press. A template is fitted into the end of the tool, polymer clay is inserted into the cavity, and a plunger forces the polymer out in a length of whatever shape template you've used. A selection of a dozen or more templates provides a variety of shapes to use for many decorative purposes.

There are a variety of things that can serve as your work surface. Look for something that cleans easily, doesn't scratch, and is a neutral color. A ceramic tile from the hardware store is ideal; a slab of marble or sheet of glass will work, too. (If you're using glass, have the sharp edges polished at the glass

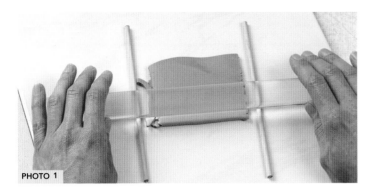

PHOTO 1

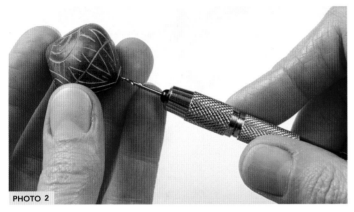

PHOTO 2

store, or cover them with electrical or duct tape.) I like to use a piece of waxed paper on top of my work surface, so I can easily move project components. A cutting blade is a necessity for almost any polymer clay project. There are blades sold specifically for polymer clay, but surgical tissue blades or paint scraper blades also work very well; look for these blades in 3- to 6-inch (7.6 to 15.2 cm) lengths, depending on the type you buy. Standard razor blades are generally not long enough to work well.

One very simple way to create beads of uniform size is to use small canapé cutters to cut shapes from a sheet of clay.

If the sheet is of uniform thickness, each of these shapes will yield the same size bead. You can make beads of graduated size by using multiples of the cutout shape, one for a small bead, one and a half for the next size bead, and so on.

A craft knife (for other kinds of cutting) and a *needle tool* (for poking holes) are also items that should find their way into your collection of polymer clay tools. Bamboo skewers and steel weaving needles both work well for suspending beads while they're baking, so the beads won't get a flat spot on the bottom. Bamboo skewers will not last for more than two or three bakings, in my experi-

ence, before they become difficult to remove from the bead. For smaller holes, you can bake beads on T-pins or quilting pins, sticking the tip of the pin into an upside-down aluminum pie pan. It's also possible to bake on polyester batting for shapes that need cushioning. When making a hole in an unbaked bead, minimize distortion by rotating the piercing tool as you push it through the bead. Stop pushing when you see its tip coming out the other side, then pierce again from the exit hole side. Some people prefer to drill holes in the clay after baking it, to prevent any distortion to the shape or pattern. Power drills can easily get out of control on something so small as a bead, so I recommend instead that you use a pin vise, a wonderful little hand-turned drill (see photo 2). These are often available at hobby stores, the kind that cater to model railroad enthusiasts.

You can carve baked polymer clay with a *v-shaped gouge*, sold in craft stores as a linoleum block cutter. You'll also find yourself beginning to collect interesting textures to make impressions in polymer clay. Don't resist! This is part of the process.

Polymer tools and materials (l to r): cotton muslin buffing wheel, polymer clay varnish, dust/mist mask, fine-grit sandpaper, acrylic paintbrush

Glues

If it's necessary to glue polymer clay, cyanoacrylate glues tend to work best. Clean the surfaces to be glued with a quick swipe of an alcohol-soaked cotton ball to remove any oils that may prevent a good bond.

Adding Shine

After baking, you might want to add some shine to your polymer clay beads. You can achieve this in several ways. Most polymer clay manufacturers also have a varnish specifically for use on polymer. Don't be tempted to use clear nail polish or acrylic spray—these may provide a shine, but they can also begin to degrade the polymer clay, and in a week or two, you'll find the surface of the bead turning sticky.

Another option is sanding, with or without subsequent buffing. Polymer clay must be wet-sanded for a couple of reasons. First, dry sanding creates dust, and breathing that dust isn't good for us. Also, sanding will heat the surface of the polymer slightly, making it more susceptible to scratch marks from the sanding. To solve these problems, dip the sandpaper and the polymer into a bowl of water occasionally during sanding.

You can purchase wet/dry sandpaper at auto supply stores. The 320-grit grade will remove small bumps, and 400-grit is good for removing surface imperfections. As you work up to higher grits, it's important to not skip grades. Move through the 600-grit, then finish with the 800, or even 1,000-grit or higher. Of course, the smoother a piece is before baking, the less sanding you'll have to do. Sand in a circular motion or back and forth, whichever is most comfortable to you. Keep an eye on the piece as you sand; polymer clay sands very quickly, and you don't want to sand away part of your design.

After sanding, you can enhance the shine even further by buffing your beads. Rub the bead vigorously with a piece of soft denim, or use a cotton muslin buffing wheel. You can purchase a jeweler's buffing wheel through a jewelry supply store or catalog, or modify an inexpensive bench grinder from a home improvement store to accommodate a cotton wheel.

Practice safe buffing! Tie back your hair, remove dangling necklaces and bracelets, and roll up your sleeves. It's advisable to wear eye protection and a dust mask, because bits of cotton fiber from the wheel become airborne during buffing. Always hold your bead on the underside of the wheel when buffing, so if it gets snatched from your fingers, it will fly away from you. Make sure there are no children, pets, or any breakables in the line of fire. Keep your bead moving at all times on the wheel, because the friction will cause the polymer clay to melt slightly if it's held in one place too long.

PHOTO 3

Special Techniques: Blends & Canes

Learning how to create these processes will give your polymer clay pieces an intricate look that's easy to achieve.

Skinner Blends

Skinner blends are wonderful things! They're named for Judith Skinner, who first provided instructions for creating them. A Skinner blend is a subtle fade from one color to another. A pasta machine is practically a necessity for creating them; if you must use a brayer or rolling pin, the blends will take considerably longer to achieve and the transition may not be as smooth. The simplest Skinner blend uses two colors, so we'll start there.

Roll each of two colors of polymer clay into rectangular sheets of the same length and width; use the thickest setting on your pasta machine, or roll them to a thickness of $^1/_8$ inch (3 mm). Cut these sheets in half diagonally. Remove one of the triangles of each color, and create a new rectangle by placing the triangles next to each other, with their angled edges touching, then press the angled edges to each other, so they stick together. Pass them through the pasta machine (see photo 3). Fold the sheet from bottom to top, and roll it out again. (If you're using a pasta machine, be sure to insert the folded edge first.)

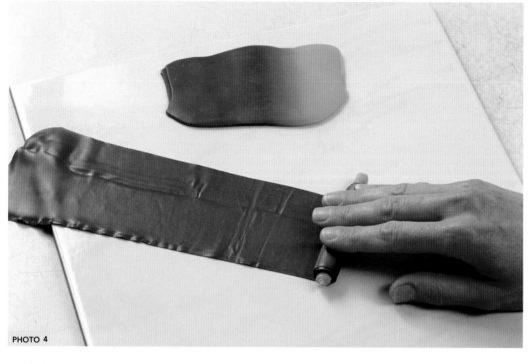

PHOTO 4

Repeat this process at least 20 times to obtain a subtle blend from one color to the other. Always fold the sheet in the same direction and, whether you're using a pasta machine or a brayer, always start rolling the sheet from the folded edge out to the open ends.

Repeated passes through the pasta machine will cause the sheet to grow wider; use your fingertip as a guide on the top of the rollers to keep the sheet at its original width. The blend is complete when you aren't able to see any lines of demarcation; the transition between colors should be smooth and uninterrupted.

Sometimes you'll use your Skinner blend in this sheet form, but for other purposes, such as caneworking, you'll roll it into a tube. To do this, turn the blend 90 degrees so that a solid color is at both the bottom and the top (don't fold it!), and pass it through the pasta machine on the next-thinnest setting. Continue to run the blended sheet through the pasta machine at smaller and smaller settings, until it's as thin as you're comfortable working with. Lay it flat on your work surface. Cut the ragged edges off one short end, and roll the polymer clay from that end into a tight roll, working slowly so that you don't incorporate any air bubbles into the tube (see photo 4).

When you've rolled the entire elongated sheet into a tube, it will be a solid color in the center and will blend into the other color as it moves outward to the perimeter . Rolling the tube so that the lighter color is in the center often creates a more dimensional effect.

Uses for Skinner blends are almost infinite; I suggest them for several of the polymer clay projects that follow. When used as components in caneworking, the resulting canes have a great deal of dimension.

Caneworking

Caneworking is perhaps the most widely recognized technique applied to polymer clay. Caneworking, or caning, is the process of layering and assembling different colors of polymer clay into a tube or rod shape, so that the tube then has an image that runs through its length. The image is revealed when the cane is sliced. The cane can be reduced in diameter by carefully rolling, stretching, and pulling it. If reduced carefully, the image within will remain intact.

Thick slices from a cane can become beads by piercing them. Thin slices may be rolled smoothly into the base bead, or left raised on the surface for an appliqué effect. Instructions for a few basic canes follow.

JELLYROLL CANE
Roll two sheets of different colors of polymer clay to approximately the same length and width. Lay one on top of the other and roll them up like a jellyroll cake. Roll carefully and snugly, and avoid capturing air bubbles in the roll. Varying the thicknesses of either of the sheets gives different effects.

BULL'S EYE CANE
Roll a short, thick tube of polymer clay (a Skinner blend, perhaps?). Roll another color of polymer into a sheet. Create a clean edge by slicing off one edge of the sheet. Place the tube on the sheet, along the cut edge, then cut the sheet to be as wide as the tube is long. Carefully roll the tube, wrapping the sheet around it. When you've rolled it far enough that the cut edge meets the rest of the sheet, roll gently to indent a line on the sheet of polymer. Roll the partially wrapped tube back just enough to be able to cut along the indentation line, then continue to wrap the tube, butting the two cut edges of the sheet together. You can repeat this with as many additional sheets of polymer to add as many rings as you'd like.

STRIPED CANE
Roll two or more sheets of polymer clay to approximately the same length and width. Stack them on top of each other, trimming the edges to make them even. Layer them carefully, to avoid trapping the dreaded air bubbles between layers. Cut the stack in half, and place one half on top of the other. Repeat until the stack is as many layers high as you want and can be comfortably worked with.

CHECKERBOARD CANE
Create a striped cane as described above, with two colors of polymer clay that are of equal thickness (it's easiest to work this technique with polymer rolled to the thickest pasta machine setting, about $^1/_8$ inch [3 mm]). Stack one on top of the other. Cut this slab into strips, each strip approximately as wide as one individual stripe. Flip every other strip over to create alternating stripes, and press them gently together to adhere them to each other. Cut the resulting slab in half crosswise and stack, to create the checkerboard pattern.

With the basic techniques of working with polymer clay under your belt, you're ready to try your hand at the fun projects that follow.

Coiled Beads

These simple beads have real impact when you choose an exciting color palette, and metallic clays have an irresistibly soft gleam. Make use of some pretty colors of scrap polymer clay; perhaps chop several colors and mix them together lightly, or even use a Skinner blend.

IRENE SEMANCHUK DEAN

Making Beautiful **Beads**

½ ounce (14 g) each of
several coordinating colors
of polymer clay; use one of
the stronger, more flexible
polymer clays
Cutting blade or craft knife
Clay gun extruder; optional
Skewers or knitting needles

PHOTO 1

INSTRUCTIONS

1. Roll same-size pieces of
polymer clay into thin
strands of uniform thickness
along their length, as shown
in photo 1. If you're using an
extruder, use one of the
round templates. The diameter of the strands will determine the size of the finished
beads. A good size to start
with is slightly less than ⅛
inch (3 mm) thick and 2 inches (5 cm) long.

2. Taper the ends of each
strand by applying slight
pressure with your fingertip
as you roll the ends against
your work surface.

3. Wind this strand around
your skewer or knitting needle. Start slightly in from the
end of the strand, and rotate
the skewer as you apply the
polymer strand. When you
reach the end, gently press
the tip onto the strand to
form a circle at the end
(see photo 2). Turn the skewer
around, and form a circle
with the end you started
with. Note that the size of
the skewer you use should
be large enough to accommodate the diameter of
the stringing material
you intend to use.

4. Rotate the skewer as you
gently apply your finger to
the outside of the coil to
smooth it.

5. Bake on the skewer at the
manufacturer's recommend-
ed temperature for 20 to 30
minutes.

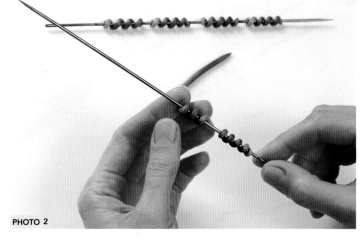

PHOTO 2

Imitation Ivory

Create some remarkable resemblances to other materials, such as ivory or bone, by studying and using traditional markings and patterns on stone, bone, or ivory from various ethnic traditions.

IRENE SEMANCHUK DEAN

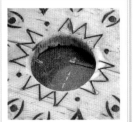

MATERIALS & TOOLS

1½ (42 g) ounces
translucent polymer clay
½ (14 g) ounce white
polymer clay
Burnt umber acrylic paint
Pasta machine or brayer
Waxed paper or
plastic wrap
Cutting blade
Small items for texturing,
such as a coffee stirring
straw, golf tee, or leather-
working stamps
Piercing tool or pin vise
Paper towels
Soft cloth or buffing wheel

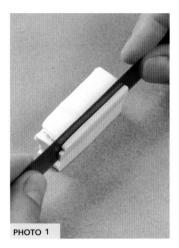

PHOTO 1

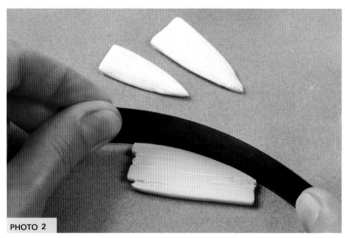

PHOTO 2

PHOTO 3

INSTRUCTIONS

1. Thoroughly mix ½ ounce (14 g) translucent polymer clay with ½ ounce (14 g) ounce white. Roll the clay into a sheet about ⅛ inch (3 mm) thick (or at the thickest setting of your pasta machine). Roll the remaining 1 ounce (28 g) of translucent clay into a sheet of the same thickness. Translucent polymer clay can very easily become overworked and sticky. If this happens, let the polymer rest and cool at any time during this project.

2. Stack one sheet on top of the other, and roll them together through the pasta machine, or with your brayer, flattening them to ⅛ inch (3 mm) thick. Cut the sheet in half, stack, and roll it again. Repeat this twice more.

3. Now cut this layered sheet into quarters, and stack them of top of each other, but roll them only enough to adhere the layers to each other; don't flatten them. Cut this stack in half, and place one half on top of the other. Your resulting layered block will be about 2 inches (5 cm) square and 1 inch (2.5 cm) high and composed of many, many thin layers.

4. Use your cutting blade to slice off one vertical end of the stack, about ⅛ inch (3 mm) thick, as shown in photo 1. Subtle striations will be visible. Lay this slice onto a piece of waxed paper. Cut it into a "tooth" shape—wider at one end, curving inward to a point—by bending your cutting blade slightly to make the curved cuts (see photo 2).

5. Place a piece of waxed paper or plastic wrap on top of the piece of polymer clay, and with your fingertip, gently coax the edges downward to bevel them. Using waxed paper or plastic wrap keeps your finger from sticking and smearing the striations.

6. Use your tiny tools to impress a pattern into the polymer clay, as shown in photo 3; be careful not to smear the layers. Study pictures of ethnic bone beads for pattern inspirations. Sharp-edged tools that cut a well-defined shape into the polymer create more realistic designs than something like a rubber stamp, which isn't as crisp.

7. You can make the bead holes at this time, or use a pin vise after baking. I prefer the latter, as it provides a more realistic effect. Bake the bead according to the manufacturer's directions.

PHOTO 4

8. When the bead is cool, drill a hole with your pin vise if you didn't make one before baking (see photo 2 on page 43). It shouldn't be necessary to sand the bead, but if there are any rough edges or burrs, sand with 600- or 800-grit wet/dry sandpaper, just enough to smooth the rough spot.

9. Referring to photos 4 and 5, rub burnt umber acrylic paint onto the bead, pressing the paint into all the indentations, then immediately wipe away the excess paint from the surface with a paper towel. Buff the bead with a soft cloth, or very lightly on a buffing wheel. Buffing the bead with very little or no prior sanding creates a soft sheen, giving your faux ivory beads a more realistic look.

PHOTO 5

Faux Stone Pendant

Strong Mayan motifs are incised into these luminous, stonelike pieces. Tinted translucent polymer clay helps you to create the look of exotic stone. This same technique can be used with other contrasting colors of polymer clay and paint, to imitate a variety of natural materials.

IRENE SEMANCHUK DEAN

MATERIALS & TOOLS

2 ounces (56 g) translucent polymer clay

Small amount (walnut-sized) piece of olive green polymer clay, for "jade"

Black and/or verdigris embossing powder (available where rubber stamping supplies are sold)

Raw sienna acrylic paint

Gold-colored wire, 18- or 20-gauge

Accent beads

Waxed paper or plastic wrap

Acrylic roller, or printer's brayer

Soft-tipped sculpting tool; optional

Small v-shaped gouge, such as a linoleum block cutter or veiner

Rag or cloth

Paper towel

Wet/dry sandpaper, 400–800 grit

Buffing wheel with cotton muslin wheel, or soft denim cloth

Round-nose jewelry pliers

INSTRUCTIONS

1. Divide your translucent polymer clay into three or four parts, slightly unequal in size. Mix varying amounts of olive green polymer into each piece of the translucent clay, so you'll have a range of shades. Start

PHOTO 1

PHOTO 2

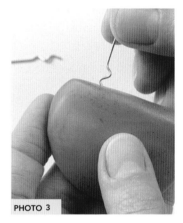

PHOTO 3

with very small amounts of green—you can always add more if it's not dark enough. Mix a pinch of the embossing powders into one or two of the shades of the tinted translucent polymer (see photo 1).

2. Combine the various shades of polymer into one clump, and mix them together slightly, leaving the colors variegated. Be careful not to incorporate air bubbles as you mix the shades together. Translucent polymer can easily become overworked, so if it seems too squishy, let it rest until it firms up a bit.

3. Cut a piece of the clay the size you'd like your pendant to be. Roll it in your hands gently to form a ball, then lightly roll it side to side, to make the ball oval-shaped.

4. Place this oval onto a piece of waxed paper, and press down with your palm to

flatten it slightly. Use a brayer or acrylic roller to roll the polymer from side to side, so that the back of the piece becomes flattened against the work surface, and the front of the piece is curved, as shown in photo 2. Shape it by tamping the top and bottom with your fingers. If you cover the polymer with a piece of plastic wrap or waxed paper, you'll be able to shape and smooth it without leaving any fingerprints.

5. Cut two pieces of wire, each 3 inches (7.6 cm) long. Use the pliers to bend a gentle back-and-forth squiggle in one end of each piece, as shown in photo 3. Push one end of each wire into the top of the pendant, so the wires are evenly spaced from each side. Use your finger or a soft-tipped sculpting tool to press the polymer back into place around the wire. The bends in the wires will keep

them from pulling out of the polymer after it's baked.

6. Peel the waxed paper from the back of the polymer, place the pendant-to-be onto a baking sheet or tile, and bake at the manufacturer's recommended temperature for a full 30 to 40 minutes. Allow it to cool completely.

7. When the piece has cooled, sand it with 400-grit wet/dry sandpaper, then let it dry thoroughly. Create the design shown (or create your own) by drawing it directly

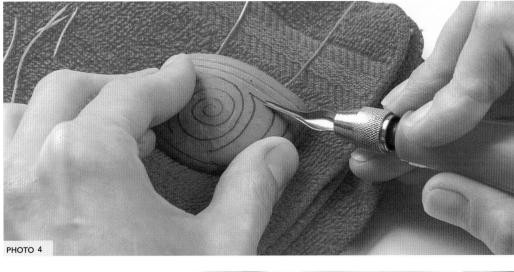

PHOTO 4

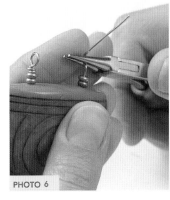

PHOTO 6

onto the polymer with a pencil or ballpoint pen.

8. Set the pendant onto a piece of cloth or a rag so it doesn't slip as you carve it. Use the v-shaped gouge to slowly and carefully incise along the lines you've drawn (see photo 4).

To carve curved lines, it's often easier to hold the gouge in place and move the polymer under it, instead of trying to move the gouge in that direction. Carve slowly and deliberately; don't rush this part! Hold the tool carefully so that if it slips, the gouge isn't pointed directly at your fingers. Brush away the polymer shavings as they accumulate. You can sand off the pencil markings and redraw lines at any time if you desire.

9. When the carving is complete, wet-sand it with 400-grit sandpaper, to remove

PHOTO 5

any burrs and remaining pen or pencil marks. Dry the bead thoroughly.

10. As shown in photo 5, use your fingertips to rub burnt sienna acrylic paint into your carving. Push the paint into the carved lines to ensure that it gets into every element of the design. Wipe

off the excess paint with a paper towel. Don't worry about removing every bit; you'll sand it off later.

11. Allow the paint to dry completely; overnight is best. Sand your pendant with 400-, 600-, then 800-grit wet/dry sandpaper.

12. Add some coordinating accent beads onto each of the wires. Use your round-nose pliers to create a loop in each wire at the top (see photo 6), to accommodate a cord. Snip off the excess wire.

13. Buff the pendant on a piece of soft denim or on a cotton buffing wheel. Be careful not to catch the wire in the fast-moving wheel.

Inside-Out Bead

The intricate detail in these beads is created by using the random pattern that results from a deceptively simple technique.

IRENE SEMANCHUK DEAN

MATERIALS & TOOLS

2 ounces (56 g) polymer clay in three to six coordinating colors (this is a great project to use up odds and ends from other projects; Skinner blend scraps are especially effective)

1 ounce (28 g) black (or other color) polymer clay, for accent

Waxed paper

Rolling pin or brayer

Cutting blade

Craft knife

Needle tool for piercing

Wet/dry sandpaper, 400–800 grit

Coarse sandpaper, 40- to 60-grit, or other texturing material

INSTRUCTIONS

1. Combine the various coordinating colors of polymer clay (but not the accent color) into a wad that is the approximate size you'd like your finished bead to be. Squeeze to adhere, but don't blend the colors. Roll this wad of polymer into a short tube.

2. Hold one end of the tube between your fingers, and with the other hand, twist the rest of it, as shown in photo 1. The colors will be spiraled like those on a barber pole.

PHOTO 1

3. Roll the tube under your fingers, on your work surface, to smooth it and make it a uniform thickness. Spiralling and rolling will lengthen the tube of polymer. Push the ends back toward the center to make it bead-sized. Use your brayer or rolling pin to square off the sides. Flip several times to ensure even shaping. Make the edges of the tube very square by using a gentle pinching motion to pull them into a slight ridge (see photo 2). Lessen the exaggeration of these edges by rolling the sides once or twice more with your brayer.

4. Cut lengthwise through the center of the squared-off tube. Let the halves fall open; notice the mirror image pattern. Cut each of these halves lengthwise down the center, again allowing those portions to fall open, as shown in photo 3. If you don't like the patterns that are revealed, push the polymer back together and start over.

PHOTO 2

5. Reassemble the pieces, so that their inside faces are now on the outside. These newly cut surfaces show mirror-image patterns; align the pattern when you're reassembling the bead. Smooth the seams with short, gentle strokes of your fingertip, being careful not to smear the design.

6. Use your brayer or rolling pin to smooth and resquare the bead. Slice off the distorted ends. Pierce the bead lengthwise, and bake for 20 to 30 minutes at the manufacturer's recommended temperature. Wet-sand and buff the cooled bead if desired.

7. Roll the black polymer clay into a sheet approximately $1/16$ inch (1.5 mm) thick. Place it on a piece of waxed paper, and press a piece of coarse sandpaper onto the surface of the polymer for texture. Flip the sheet of polymer over so that the textured side is down. Set one of the pierced ends of

PHOTO 3

the baked bead onto the sheet of black polymer, and cut around the perimeter to make a bead cap (see photo 4). Pull away the excess black polymer, then peel the waxed paper from the end of the bead. Repeat on the other end.

8. Smooth the bead cap into place around the edges, and use the coarse sandpaper to retexture any area that needs it. Pierce the bead caps and rebake the bead for 20 minutes at the manufacturer's recommended temperature.

PHOTO 4

IRENE SEMANCHUK DEAN

Textured Skinner Blend Whorls

These textured, organic forms display the softly subtle graduated colors of a Skinner blend. Their shapes recall the graceful whorl of a snail's shell.

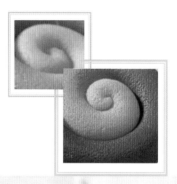

PHOTO 1

PHOTO 2

INSTRUCTIONS

1. Cut two strips ¼ inch (6 mm) wide from the blended
sheet (see photo 1). Cut along the blended edge; that is, your
strips should be a different color on each end, blending in
the middle.

2. Roll one of the strips on your work surface with your
fingers, until its squared shape becomes rounded. Roll gently,
pushing in from either end if the tube starts to get elongated.
Roll each strip to equal length; 2 inches (5 cm) long is a good
size to start with. Taper one end of each by applying slight
pressure to it as you roll the polymer clay under your
fingertips.

3. Place each tube on a sheet of coarse-grit sandpaper, and
roll it gently back and forth, to texture the polymer completely.

4. Hold the textured piece of polymer in one hand and,
with the fingers of your other hand, begin to roll the tapered
edge inward, similar to a snail shell, as shown in photo 2.
Roll it completely around to the end, pressing gently to
adhere the polymer to itself without flattening the texture.

5. Pierce the spiraled bead from one side to the other, as
shown in photo 3. Pierce with a very thin needle tool or
straight pin to avoid exiting the polymer in the middle of
the bead where it's thinnest. If you do poke a hole through
the side of the middle, remove the piercing tool, unspiral
your bead, and start again. Tamp the bead gently on the
sandpaper to retexture it, if necessary.

6. Bake at the manufacturer's recommended temperature
for 20 to 30 minutes.

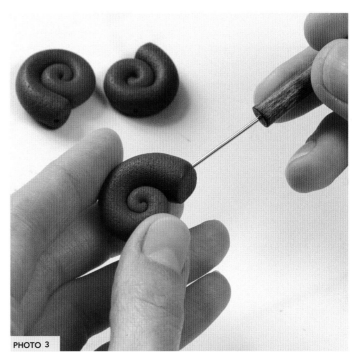

PHOTO 3

Layered Translucent Canes

The vibrant pattern in these gleaming beads is highlighted by minute layers of black and white polymer in translucent canes. Simpler cane designs work better with this technique.

IRENE SEMANCHUK DEAN

MATERIALS & TOOLS

2 ounces (56 g) translucent polymer clay

Small amounts of various colors polymer clay

½ ounce (14 g) each black and white polymer clay

1 to 2 ounces (28 to 56 g) white or light-colored scrap polymer clay

Rolling pin or brayer

Pasta machine; optional

Cutting blade

Alcohol

Needle tool for piercing

Flat object, such as a small piece of glass or clear acrylic sheet

Wet/dry sandpaper, 400– 800– or 1000–grit

Cotton muslin buffing wheel; optional

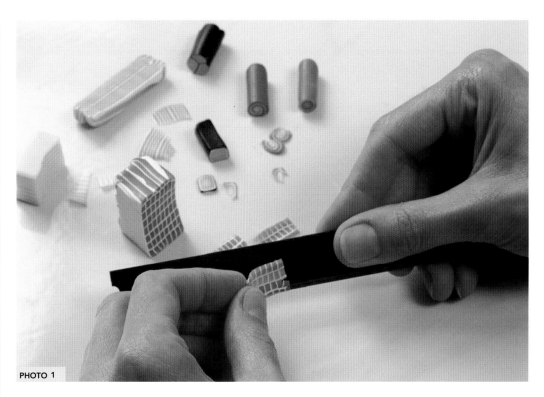

PHOTO 1

INSTRUCTIONS

1. Separate the translucent polymer into three or four sections, and tint all but one of the sections by adding small amounts of colored polymer to them. Add a small amount at a time, because too much will increase the opacity.

PHOTO 2

2. Following the caneworking instructions on page 47, use tinted and regular translucent polymer to create several small simple canes. Use very thin sheet elements in black and white, for highlighting.

3. Allow the canes to rest and firm up; translucent clay can easily become overworked and squishy. If possible, allow them to rest overnight. In the meantime, form base beads with white or light-colored scrap polymer clay. You'll be adding several thin layers to each bead, so they'll end up being a bit larger than your original base bead.

4. When the canes are cool and firm, use a very sharp cutting blade to remove extremely thin slices (see photo 1). Clean the blade between each slice on a paper towel with a bit of rubbing alcohol on it. The slices you remove should be as thin as you can possibly cut them— thinner than paper. This will take practice! Rarely will you be able to cut a complete slice—most will be partial slices, and that's very much all right for this project.

If any slices are too thick, you can pass them through

continued

your pasta machine at the thinnest setting. If they want to stick to the rollers of the pasta machine, dust the rollers very lightly with cornstarch to prevent sticking.

5. Apply the slices randomly to the surface of your base bead (see photo 2 on page 61). When you've applied one layer, roll the bead gently in your cupped palms to smooth the cane slices into the bead. Roll gently to avoid smearing the cane designs. Apply more slices, overlapping the previous ones. Continue applying slices and rolling to smooth for another layer or two.

6. To create a bicone-shaped bead, set a round bead on your clean work surface. Place a flat object—a jar lid will work, but I prefer a piece of clear acrylic sheet that I can see through—on top of the bead, and use it to roll the bead on your work surface, using a gentle, circular motion. Tilt the acrylic sheet slightly as you roll and you'll see the bicone shape begin to form, as shown in photo 3.

PHOTO 3

Notice that the angle at which you hold the sheet controls how pointed the bicone will be. Reverse the direction of your circular motion to prevent the cane design from spiraling at the tips of the bicone. Roll it only enough to create the desired shape. Too much rolling will distort your beautiful translucent cane patterns!

7. Pierce the beads through the bicone tips or, if you prefer, from side to side. Bake at the manufacturer's recommended temperature for 30 minutes.

8. When the beads are finished baking, immediately immerse them in a sink or bowl of ice water. There is some evidence that sudden quick-cooling increases the polymer's translucence.

9. When the beads have cooled, sand their surfaces thoroughly with 400- through 800- or 1000-grit wet/dry sandpaper. Buffing on a cotton buffing wheel will increase the translucence and add depth to your patterns.

Mokume Gane

IRENE SEMANCHUK DEAN

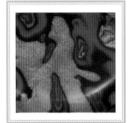

The Japanese term mokume gane *means* "wood in metal." *The wood-grain look is particularly beautiful if you use metallic polymer clays, or tinted translucents layered with ultra thin metal leaf.*

MATERIALS & TOOLS

1 ounce (28 g) each of three colors of polymer clay

Rolling pin, brayer, or pasta machine

Waxed paper

Variety of items for making deep impressions in polymer clay, such as golf tee, canapé cutter, or pen cap

Cutting blade

Rubbing alcohol

Needle tool for piercing

Wet/dry sandpaper, 400–800 grit

Buffing wheel equipped with cotton muslin wheel, or piece of soft denim; optional

PHOTO 1

PHOTO 2

PHOTO 3

INSTRUCTIONS

1. Use the pasta machine or brayer to roll out several uniformly thin sheets of each color of polymer clay to $1/16$ inch (1.6 mm) thick. If you're not using a pasta machine, you might not be able to achieve such thin sheets, but that's ok.

2. Cut the sheets of polymer clay into several 2 x 3-inch (5 x 7.6 cm) rectangles, and layer eight to 12 of them on top of each other, alternating colors (see photo 1). As you add each sheet, roll it gently with the brayer to ensure good adhesion with the layer below. Apply pressure as you roll the brayer to flatten and enlarge the stack to $1/4$ inch (6 mm). Flip the stack occasionally as you roll to ensure even distribution.

3. Use your small tools to make deep impressions in the stack of polymer clay. You can space them evenly or randomly, or even overlap them, as shown in photo 2.

4. Press the stack firmly to your work surface so that it's well adhered and doesn't move. Referring to photo 3, hold your cutting blade at each end, parallel to the top of the stack, and draw it across the top of the stack, removing a thin layer of polymer. You probably won't be able to remove a piece the size of the entire top of the stack; that's okay—it adds to the organic appearance of the design. Wipe your blade with a bit of rubbing alcohol on a paper towel between each slice. This important step ensures clean cuts that won't drag on the layer below. Repeat this process until you have an assortment of patterned sheets. Note that the pattern is slightly different on each side, so you can use whichever side you prefer.

5. Form some round bead shapes with scrap clay. If you used translucent polymer to make your mokume gane, the base beads should be a light color, to enhance the translucence.

6. Apply the patterned sheets to your beads, as shown in photo 4, then roll them gently in the cupped palms of your hands, so that the patterned sheets are smooth and even with the surface of the bead. You can tear or cut the sheets—or even overlap them—to completely cover the bead. To make a bicone bead, follow the instructions in step 6 of the Layered Translucent Bead on page 63.

PHOTO 4

7. Bake the bead according to the manufacturer's recommended instructions. Wet-sand the beads, starting with 400-grit sandpaper, and finishing with 800- or 1,000-grit. Buff if desired; buffing increases the shine of metallic or translucent polymer clays.

I rene Semanchuk Dean has been working with polymer clay since 1992. She holds membership in the National Polymer Clay Guild, the Southern Highland Craft Guild, and is a founding member and current president of the Blue Ridge Polymer Clay Guild. She's the author of *The Weekend Crafter: Polymer Clay*, published by Lark Books (2000), and her work has been featured in six other Lark books.

Irene sells her work through her Web site, www.good-night-irene.com, as well as at art and craft shows and galleries. She teaches classes through regional polymer clay guilds.

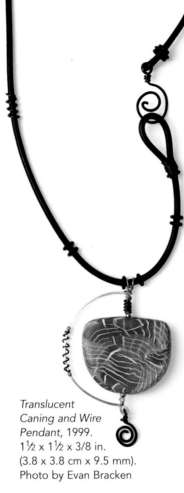

Translucent Caning and Wire Pendant, 1999. 1½ x 1½ x 3/8 in. (3.8 x 3.8 cm x 9.5 mm). Photo by Evan Bracken

Irene's recent work reflects the intermeshing of ancient and contemporary cultures, blending imagery from ancient Africa, Egypt, and Mexico with references to nature, current technological and industrial designs, and the occasional allusion to outer space. Because her work is both decorative and functional, it includes forms such as wall pieces, clocks, mirrors, light switch plates, pens, and letter openers.

Irene Semanchuk Dean
IRENE SEMANCHUK DEAN

Taliswoman Pendant, 2001. 3 x 1 x ½ in. (7.6 x 2.5 1.3 cm). Photo by Evan Bracken

Neo-Fossil Key Ring, 2001. 1½ x 1½ x 3/8 in. (3.8 x 3.8 cm x 9.5 mm). Photo by Evan Bracken

Polymer Clay
GALLERY

Butterfly Wing and Quill Patterned Beads, Desiree McCrorey, 2001. 1½ x ¾ in. (3.8 x 1.9 cm). Photo by Liv Ames

Big Bead Series: Zuni Turquoise Bear Fetish, Diane W. Villano, 2001. 7¼ x 4½ x 2¼ in. (18.4 x 11.4 x 5.7 cm). Photo by William K. Sacco

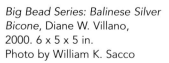

Big Bead Series: Balinese Silver Bicone, Diane W. Villano, 2000. 6 x 5 x 5 in. Photo by William K. Sacco

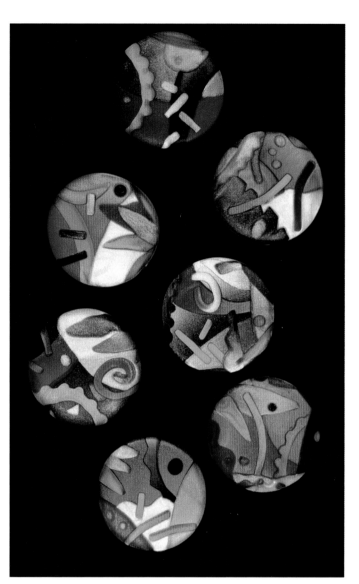

Earth Tone Composition Beads, Dorothy Greynolds, 2001. 1 x 1 x ⅜ in. (2.5 x 2.5 x 1 cm). Photo by artist

Shoe and Purse Beads, Deborah Anderson, 2001. Left: ½ x ½ x 1 in. (1.3 x 1.3 x 2.5 cm); right: ¼ x 1 x 1 in. (.6 x 2.5 x 2.5 cm). Photo by Liv Ames

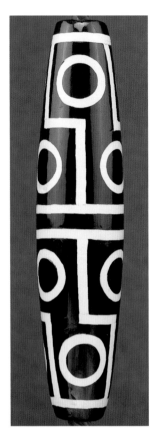

Big Bead Series: Inlaid dZi Bead, Diane W. Villano, 2001. 6¼ x 1¼ x 1¼ in. (15.9 x 3.1 x 3.1 cm). Photo by William K. Sacco

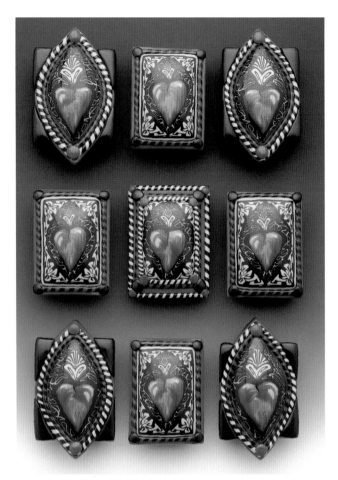

Heart Beads, Sarah Nelson Shriver, 1999. 1¼ x ¾ x ½ in. (3.1 x 1.9 x 1.3 cm). Photo by George Post

Girl with Bird II, Cynthia Toops, 1996. 2½ x 1 x 1 in. (6.4 x 2.5 x 2.5 cm). Polymer clay over glass core by Dan Adams. Photo by Robert K. Liu

Totem Beads, Patricia Kimle, 2000. 4½ x 1½ x ½ inch (11.4 x 3.8 x 1.3 cm). Photo by artist

Primary Beads, Cynthia Pack, 2001. 1 x 1 x 1 in. (2.5 x 2.5 x 2.5 cm). Photo by artist

Untitled,
Cynthia
Toops, 1998.
2 x 1¼ x ¾ in.
(5 x 3.1 x 1.9 cm).
Photo by Roger Schreiber

Fancy Leaves Pendants (detail), Patricia Kimle, 2001. 3 x 1½ x ¾ inch (7.6 x 3.8 x 1.9 cm).
Photo by artist

Blue and Green Inspirational Beads, Cynthia Pack, 2001. 1 x 1 x 1 in. (2.5 x 2.5 x 2.5 cm).
Photo by artist

Introduction to Metal

BY JOANNA GOLLBERG

Metal is a wonderful material, and metal beads have been made throughout the ages in every culture. There are many different types of nonferrous metals that you can work with to create metal beads. In this chapter, we'll use brass, copper, sterling silver (92.5 percent fine silver and 7.5 percent copper), and fine silver (99.9 percent silver). These metals vary in color and can be mixed for further interesting effects. We'll explore some of the modern techniques— as well as some ancient ones— used in metal bead making.

Metal for bead making comes in sheets, tubes, and wire.

The Basics

These are the basic materials you'll use to create metal beads. As you progress, you'll add more items to your basic kit of metalwork materials.

Finding Metal

Nonferrous metal (metal not containing iron) of all kinds is available through jewelry supply houses. Most of the beads made with the hot tools are done in sterling silver. It comes in a variety of versatile forms; for the projects shown here, sheet, wire, and tubing were used. Metal sheet and wire are measured in a standard gauge system, called "B & S" after Mr. Brown and Mr. Sharp, the system's developers. The diameter of tubing is measured in millimeters or fractions of an inch. (Gauges may differ slightly, depending on the manufacturer, but not enough to really matter to us while making beads.) A gauge indicates the metal's thickness inversely: the higher the gauge number, the thinner the metal. Sheet metal is obviously always flat, but you can order it in many precut shapes, such as round discs. Wire comes in many shapes, such as round, square, half-round, triangular, and bar. We'll work with round wire in this chapter, but if you want to experiment with other wire shapes, please do.

A variety of files, hammers and mallets, jeweler's saw (resting on a bench pin), flexible shaft drill

Solder & Flux

Solder allows you to join two separate pieces of metal together. Solder comes in sheet, wire, and paste forms, but I strongly suggest using wire solder. No matter what type you use, solder is rated according to its melting point. You use more than one grade of solder when you'll be soldering in stages, so that a previous joint can stand up to subsequent exposure to the torch without coming apart. Hard solder melts at 1365° F (740° C), medium at 1275° F (690° C), and easy at 1240° F (671° C). *Flux* is a type of salt used in the soldering process that helps solder to flow. Apply flux with an inexpensive hair-bristle paintbrush.

Tools

There are two ways of working with metals. Cold metalwork involves cutting, piercing, and bending, while hot work means using a torch to join pieces. You'll need two sets of basic tools, but I'm including only the necessary tools for each type of metalworking presented here. All of these tools can be purchased at jewelry supply houses.

COLD TOOLS

The *flexible shaft drill* is an electric jeweler's tool, similar to a drill, and is capable of variable speeds, like a sewing machine or an automobile's gas pedal. It has a long, flexible shaft that attaches the motor to the handpiece, and it's very convenient for making jewelry. The handpiece has a chuck, smaller than that of an ordinary household drill, which holds small accessories, such as drill bits. Another option is to use a multipurpose electric hand tool (available at home improvement centers) with its own flexible shaft attachment. The accessories offered with this type of drill will perform the same functions as a jeweler's drill.

There are countless flex shaft accessories and drill bits available on the market that will help you pierce, sand, and polish metal. We'll use the flex shaft mostly for drilling, sanding, and final finishes.

A jeweler's saw frame is one of the most important tools in making jewelry. There are many kinds of saw frames available, but you'll only need a basic saw frame, so use one with a standard 80-millimeter throat. There are also many sizes and kinds of saw blades available to fit the frame. I suggest using size 3/0 saw blades for most jewelry work (the 3/0 blades have finer teeth than the 2/0 or 1/0 blades) except in rare circumstances when I need an even smaller blade. The 3/0 blades remove very little metal and are strong and easy to work with. Go ahead and invest in a good quality blade, as the poor quality blades, though less expensive, are weak and prone to break. You'll do your sawing at a table or workbench with a *bench pin*.

This wooden rectangle extends from the edge of the work surface and has a deep v-shaped opening at one end. The bench pin's design allows you to support the metal piece while you work on it from a variety of angles. The chasing hammer is smaller than a household hammer and is specially weighted for use in jewelry making. One side of this ball peen ham-

Cold tools are used to shape, cut, and mark the metal.

mer's head looks like a ball, and the other has a flat face like a regular hammer.

A wooden hammer or rawhide mallet can form metal without distorting the metal surface. Either type is larger than a typical household hammer.

Use needle files to file small parts. They're perfect for making jewelry because you can file in hard-to-reach places. The round, half-round, square, triangular, and barrette needle files work well for the projects in this book. The files look exactly like their names, except for the barrette file, which is flat on one side and has no teeth on its triangular side. Pick up the large *bastard file* inexpensively at any hardware store. It should be fairly coarse, yet you should be able to run your fingers along it without your skin catching on the teeth.

A scribe is a pointed metal "pencil," used to draw or scratch on metal. You can purchase a scribe, or you can file the end of a coat hanger or a nail to a sharp point to make your own. A punch can be any kind of tool with a point on one end and a place to hammer on the other. It's used to make dimples (as decorative marks) or for drilling.

The flat nose pliers's inside surfaces are flat and meet at a flat angle on the outside of the noses. Chain nose pliers are flat on the inside and round on the outside, tapering almost to a point. Round nose pliers are completely round, also tapering to a point. Pliers-style metal snips are used to cut wire and solder.

Any piece of flat, smooth, polished steel works as a steel block. A classic jeweler's steel block can be purchased quite inexpensively from any jewelry supply house.

A *mandrel* is anything you can wrap metal around. Some mandrels are tapered, such as ring and bracelet mandrels, and some are the same diameter for the whole length. You can use anything you find around your house for a mandrel, but ring and bracelet mandrels are only available through jewelry supply houses. A *dapping block* is a cube with various sizes of concave depressions sunk into each side and is used to make domes from flat pieces of metal. The dapping block has the female depression, and the *dap* is its male counterpart. Wooden dapping blocks are less expensive than steel ones and come with two universal daps, but they have shallower depressions. You must purchase individual rather than universal steel daps, which are precisely matched to the steel block's depressions.

Steel chasing tools, used to make impressions into metal, can be round, square, or have an endless variety of shapes carved into the end.

Wet/dry sandpaper works best for sanding metal. The higher its number, the finer the grit. Use the gray kind in 220- and 400-grits; the grit in brown sandpaper isn't glued on very well and isn't suited for metalwork.

A stainless steel ruler should have a straight edge that isn't nicked or chipped, and should be marked in inches and millimeters. Shatterproof safety glasses should fit well on your face.

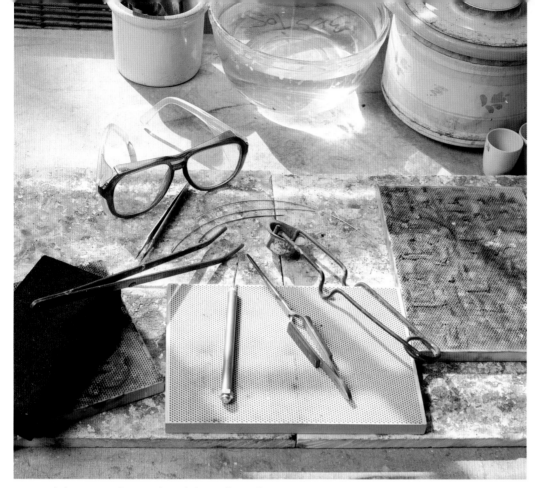

Hot tools let you work securely with heated metal.

Torch and fire extinguisher

HOT TOOLS

A torch is made up of the gas tank, the regulator, the hose, the handpiece, and the nozzle. Although you have a choice of tank fuels, such as acetylene, propane, oxygen/acetylene, or oxygen/propane, a good type of torch for a beginning jewelry maker is an acetylene "B" tank; be sure to use the proper fittings and the smallest nozzle available. I like acetylene for indoor use, because leaking gas from an acetylene tank will dissipate into the air. Gas leaking from a propane tank will gather and "hide" in a corner or behind a door, and can make a small explosion if accidentally ignited.

There are many kinds of handpieces available on the market, and they're designed to fit on specific kinds of gas tanks. In addition, the nozzles come with many sizes of openings. I suggest shopping for a tank and its fittings at a welding supply store; the whole outfit is less expensive through these dealers. Test all your connections with soapy water before using the tank to make sure it doesn't leak. If the soap bubbles up, return the tank to the supplier and exchange it for another. For important information on testing, see page 000.

A fire extinguisher is an absolutely necessary safety precaution. Purchase one at any hardware store. You should keep your fire extinguisher right next to your torch and always in the same place.

Soldering blocks are available as honeycomb ceramic and compressed charcoal blocks. Both types of materials reflect heat and are longlasting. For extra fire protection, I suggest you also use a heat-resistant board under your soldering block.

Tweezers are used to pick up hot pieces of metal. The cross-locking tweezers with wooden handles allow you to safely hold on to a piece while you're soldering it. A solder pick is made of titanium and won't stick to solder. It's an excellent tool for moving and picking up small pieces of solder.

Pickle is a weak acid used for cleaning nonferrous metals. Use copper tongs to remove items from the pickle; for important information about metal reactivity in pickling solutions, see page 104..

Basic Techniques: Moving the Metal

This chapter is organized so that you'll start by making simple beads with the cold tools and then move onto more advanced techniques that employ both the hot and cold tools. Here I'll introduce some general techniques that must be discussed before beginning your bead making.

Cutting, Piercing & Sawing

These are the most basic techniques you'll need to learn, and they'll allow you to cut shapes from sheet metal, cut lengths of tubing, and make fancy openwork designs, such as those on the Appliquéd Hollow Beads on page 90. Some sheet metal is so lightweight that you can cut it with snips, but most of the time you'll use the jeweler's saw.

Open the jaw of your saw frame so that it's ³/₈ inch (9.5 mm) shorter than the length of your saw blade. Insert the saw blade in the top nut of the frame, with the teeth facing toward you and pointing down, then tighten the nut. Rest the frame's handle on your sternum, with the top part against the side of the worktable or bench. Lean in with your sternum, shortening the length of the jaw a tiny bit, then put the end of the blade into the lower nut and tighten it; release the pressure. The blade should be very taut in the frame.

When sawing metal, move the saw frame up and down, and be sure to always keep the frame at a 90-degree angle to the metal. You should keep the frame pointing forward at all times. When rounding a corner or sawing an arcing line, turn only the metal, not the frame (unless you're turning a sharp corner; then, simultaneously turn the saw—moving it up and down quickly—*and* the metal). Most important, hold the saw lightly in your hand, letting the saw teeth do the work on the downward stroke. Use your hand simply to guide the saw, not to apply pressure. A beginner will most likely break a few saw blades. Don't fret if this happens to you—it's normal. You'll become quite proficient with a little practice.

Using the Torch

Soldering is a necessary skill for making the beads in this book. With a little practice you'll find that you soon gain confidence. Soldering should be done in a well-ventilated space. I solder in front of a window that has a strong window fan that draws the air outside, but an overhead exhaust hood provides the best ventilation. To begin, turn on the torch a little bit, and light it with a striker. (A lighter is a combustible

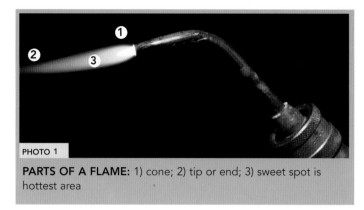

PHOTO 1

PARTS OF A FLAME: 1) cone; 2) tip or end; 3) sweet spot is hottest area

source of fuel that could be dangerous around the torch, so I recommend you use a striker instead.) Now play with the knob on the handpiece, turning the flame up and down, until you feel you understand the tension in the knob and how it relates to the flame. The hottest part of the flame is the part that comes right after the blue cone, as shown in photo 1.

Don't touch the flame's blue cone to the metal because there's a small vacuum inside the blue cone that has no heat in it. Place scrap pieces of copper, silver, and brass on your soldering block, and practice putting the heat on the metal. Slowly melt each piece to get an idea of how each kind of metal reacts to the heat.

Soldering

A solder joint is a place where two pieces of metal are permanently joined. Before you can solder a joint, you must first apply flux to the metal. Flux does two things: It allows solder to flow by keeping the metal clean (that is, free of the oxidizing effects of the torch), and it acts as a temperature indicator. When flux is heated to the point where it becomes glassy looking, the metal is usually hot enough to solder. (If overheated, flux can burn off, and you'll need to reflux your piece, because solder won't flow on a dirty piece of metal.) In order for the solder to work properly, both pieces of the joint must be at equal temperatures.

The three grades of solder—hard, medium, and easy—allow you to perform multiple soldering operations on one piece without inadvertently melting the previous soldering operation. Practice melting solder on scrap metal, and then practice soldering two pieces of metal together, first side by side, and then one piece on top of the other.

When soldering, you can use the stick solder method, or cut the wire solder into small chips, called paillons; see photo

2. Most people are taught to solder by using pallions, but the stick method works just as well and will save you a lot of time. To stick solder, cut 12 inches (30.5 cm) of solder, remembering to mark the end of your solder so you know what temperature it is. (I bend the end of easy solder into an "L," medium solder into a "U," and hard solder into a square.)

Heat the fluxed metal until the flux becomes glassy looking, then briefly touch the end of the stick of solder to the joint you want to connect. This takes some practice. At first you might get large globs of solder on the piece, but after a few times you'll be able to place just the right amount of solder where it's needed. I highly recommend this stick-soldering technique—I use it for 90 percent of all my soldering operations. I only use the pallions for very tiny soldering jobs, such as earposts and jump ring joints.

Pickling

When almost any metal is heated, it becomes black from oxidation. Oxidation results when oxygen forms oxides on the surface of the metal, appearing as a black surface layer on the metal. You can easily remove it by soaking the metal in pickle. Pickle will also remove any dried flux on your piece, so you'll need to pickle the piece after each soldering operation in order to clean the metal and prepare it for more soldering or for finishing. To make pickle, fill a container with water (I use a small electric slow cooker because hot pickle works best), then add the manufacturer's recommended amount of pickling compound to it. Always add the acid to the water—a messy reaction could occur if water is added to acid instead. I keep my pickle and a bowl of clean water right next to my soldering station, so I can quickly pickle my work and immediately rinse it after pickling. It's not a good idea to put your hands in the pickle, but if some should splash on you, simply wash the splash off with cold water. (Keep baking soda on hand and use it to neutralize acid spills; also be sure to add some to the pickle before disposing of it.) The weak acid of the pickle will eventually eat holes in cloth, so wear an apron to protect your clothing.

Be careful to never put any steel in the pickle! As it cleans your metal, pickle absorbs copper ions in a saturated solution. When steel is put into a pickle solution, an electrical charge is created that sets the ions free; these ions will migrate onto any other kind of metal that might be in the pickle, plating it with copper. To avoid accidentally copperplating a silver piece, use the copper tongs to remove all of your work from the pickle.

Annealing

When metal is worked hard, such as when wire is twisted or formed a great deal, the metal quickly becomes less malleable and is likely to break with further working. When this happens, you must *anneal* the metal before continuing. Heat the metal to almost red hot, then quench it. This realigns the molecules in the metal and makes it soft again.

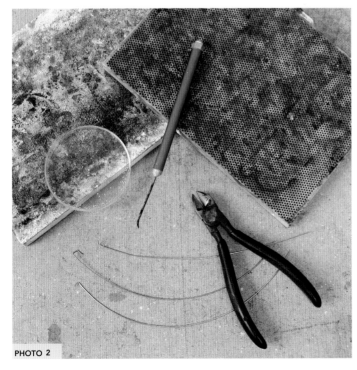

PHOTO 2

Finishing

With everything you do in metalworking, the final finish of the piece enhances and completes your design, so finishing is an important part of working with metal. When you work with the hot tools, the metal will become discolored and dirty because of contact with heat and flux. When sterling is heated during soldering, often some of the copper in the sterling alloy rises to the surface of the metal, creating a reddish undertone called firescale. Everyone whoworks with sterling silver will face the problem of firescale, but it's easily removed by sanding. Otherwise, your piece will be marred by unsightly reddish blotches.

You have several finishing options. Your piece can be matte, shiny, or have a *patina*, which is a coloration or blackening of the metal. For a matte finish, I always have on hand 400-grit wet/dry sandpaper, steel wool of various grits, and green nylon pot scrubbers. All of these materials can make a matte finish when you rub them back and forth or in a circular motion on the bead. For a shiny finish, I use a steel brush attachment in the end of the flex shaft, a polishing cloth, or a tumbler filled with steel shot. If you don't have a tumbler, the polishing cloth works great. For patinas, try selenium toner (purchased at a photographic store that sells darkroom supplies), liver of sulphur, or commercial patina products (both are available through jewelry and art supply houses). For more information on patinas, see the Rolled Bead patina variation on page 78.

There are many sanding accessories that may be used to create a final finish. Of course, hand sanding will take much longer than using a sanding accessory on a flex shaft, such as a sanding disc that snaps onto a mandrel; a split mandrel that holds a strip of sandpaper (this is what I prefer); and plastic-bristle discs. I find the bristle discs don't work well for removing metal but are fine for a final finish. Experiment with these sanding options and find which one works best for you.

Each of the projects in this chapter use some combination of the basic techniques I've introduced here. You'll see a list of "Techniques to Know" at the start of the project instructions, so you can review them if necessary.

Finally, remember that the techniques discussed for each kind of bead can be used in endless ways. Be as free and as creative as you like with these techniques! For example, use piercing and sawing on a flat disc bead, or use twisted wire on the hollow round bead. These beads are simply examples of the many creative choices available to you.

Finishes for metal include patina, matte, and shiny.

Fancy Rolled Beads

The sheet metal for this design is treated as if it's paper: folded, cut, drawn on, and colored. These beads are quick and simple to make, but with so many decorative options available, these rolled beads become intriguing little gems.

JOANNA GOLLBERG

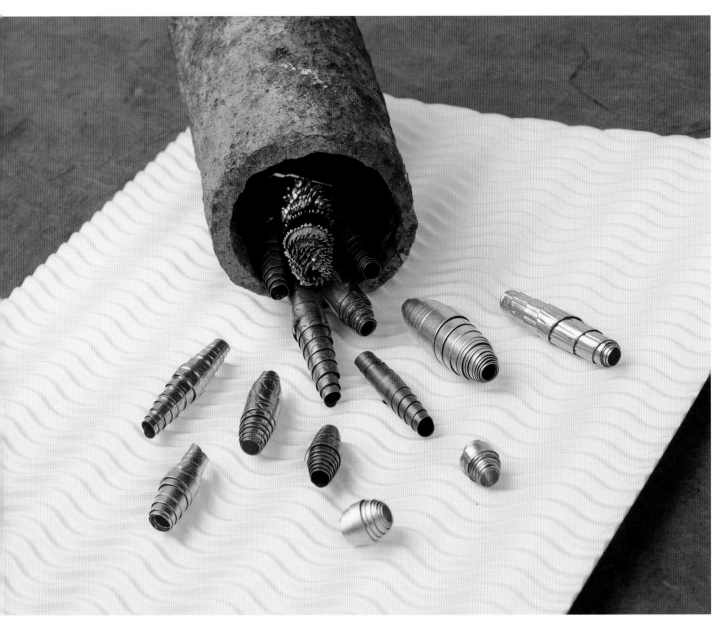

PHOTO 1

PHOTO 3

MATERIALS & TOOLS

36-gauge copper or brass
sheet metal

Metal snips or shears

Ruler

Scribe

Small round mandrel

✖ TECHNIQUES TO KNOW
Cutting, Piercing & Sawing

INSTRUCTIONS

1. Use the metal snips to cut the metal into strips 1 inch (2.5 cm) wide and 3 inches (7.6 cm) long. This basic size will help you to get an idea of what beads using longer, wider, or thinner strips will look like. The width of the strip will determine the length of the bead, and the length of the strip will decide its outer diameter. Depending on the size of your mandrel (which is used to make the hole in the bead), a piece this size will make a bead about 5 mm in diameter.

2. At one end of the strip, mark the center point with your scribe. Use this point to make a long triangle with the opposite two corners of the strip. This will be your basic plan with every bead. Using the shears, cut the triangle, rounding the corners so they aren't sharp, as shown in photo 1.

3. Place the wider end of the strip flat against a round mandrel. (A ballpoint pen is probably too big for a mandrel—the bead hole would be enormous—but a small piece of tubing or a straight piece of coat hanger would work well.) Roll the metal around the mandrel, slowly covering the widest part of the metal with the tapered end. Be sure when you roll the metal to go slow, keeping the point in the middle (see photo 2). Slide the bead off the mandrel.

Variations

Decorative Edges

Since 36-gauge metal is quite thin, try using pinking shears instead of the metal snips for a zigzag on the edges. Or use your shears to cut wavy edges, or snip short cuts for a fringe effect.

Surface Design

Using your scribe, draw designs on the triangle, making sure the design extends to the edges of the metal, because the middle of the triangle will eventually be hidden. The metal is thin and soft, and takes a design made with a pointed scribe quite nicely.

Patina

You can make the brass or copper black by dropping it into a solution of liver of sulphur. This is very simple to do and adds depth and color to your beads. If you've already added some surface design, the patina will make the surface design more apparent. (This is a smelly process, so I recommend that you do it outside or in a very well ventilated area.) Dissolve a chunk of the liver of sulphur in hot water, or follow the manufacturer's recommendations. Keep your beads in the solution until they turn black, usually one to two minutes. Don't leave the beads in the liver of sulphur for too long, because it will create a thick black crust that will flake off later. Remove the bead from the solution and wash it in *hot* water. The hot water helps the patina stay on the metal. You can leave the bead black, or rub it with an abrasive such as steel wool, scouring cleanser, or a nylon pot scrubber, to give it a nice final finish and let some of the natural color of the metal show through.

Decorative Tubes

With a variety of tube shapes and the basic techniques of piercing, sawing, and filing, this simple bead can become as fancy as you like once you start creating rich patterns on the metal.

JOANNA GOLLBERG

Copper and brass
tubing, any size
Jeweler's saw and blade
Scribe
Flexible shaft drill and drill
bits in various sizes
Needle files (round,
triangular, and barrette)

✳ **TECHNIQUES TO KNOW**
Cutting, Piercing & Sawing
Finishing

✳ **DESIGNER'S NOTE:**
Thin tubing is easily sawed
straight through, but you
should saw *around* thicker
tubing (the thicker wall has
a tendency to guide the
saw blade off on an
uneven course).

PHOTO 1

INSTRUCTIONS

1. Saw the tubing to the desired length.

2. Decide where you want your bead hole, and what size you want the hole to be. When drilling bead holes, it's best to start small, then enlarge the hole if you're stringing the bead on heavier wire or string. In all of the beads shown here, the bead holes aren't the central focus of the designs, so I positioned them as inconspicuously as possible. Use the scribe to put a small dimple on each side of the bead. This serves as a guide mark for the drill bit and helps keep the drill bit from swerving all over the surface when you're drilling. Measure carefully, because any discrepancy will be obvious once the bead is strung.

3. Drill one side of the tubing, then drill the other side. Keep the drill bit at a 90-degree angle to the tubing, as shown in photo 1. If you're feeling confident, continue through to the other side of the bead.

4. Now you can decorate your bead. You can use the saw to cut lines into the bead, or to cut the bead at different angles. Use various sizes of drill bits to drill decorative holes in your bead, or use your files to make surface decorations. The barrette file can be used to make interesting scratches on the surface, while the round and triangular files can be used to make indentations on the edges or on the surface of the tubing. The triangular file will make triangular grooves and the circular file will make half circle—shaped grooves. The designs you choose for your beads can be random or planned; both make interesting and beautiful beads.

Chased-Design Discs

The charming surface designs on these disc beads were made with chasing tools and stamps. With only one simple soldering operation, most of the work uses the cold tools. If you want to create a unique look, modify the design on a commercial stamp with files and other metalworking tools.

JOANNA GOLLBERG

MATERIALS & TOOLS

24-gauge sterling silver
discs (any diameter)
Tubing (4 millimeters or
less outside diameter)
Chasing tools and stamps
Wooden hammer or
rawhide mallet

✖ **TECHNIQUES TO KNOW**
Cutting, Piercing & Sawing
Soldering
Finishing

PHOTO 1

✖ **DESIGNER'S NOTE:**

Chasing tools are available commercially through most
jewelry supply houses, but can also be made from filing pieces of
steel you have lying around the house, such as an old screwdriver.
I have a matting tool that is actually an old flathead screwdriver
that I marred on the end. (A matting tool is a chasing tool that
makes some sort of textured design or imprint on the metal.)
Another option is to file tool steel into a design on the end, then
harden and temper it for a long-lasting, handmade chasing tool.
These handmade tools are quite fun to make, and are very satisfying to use. A huge variety of commercial stamps are also available.
Sometimes these stamps are hurriedly made, and the designs will
be uneven. If this happens, use a needle file to correct the flaw.
Keep your eye out at flea markets and junk shops for chasing tools;
they often pop up in unexpected places.

INSTRUCTIONS

1. Begin by creating a design
for the disc. This can be a
formal design or a free-form
one that uses texture from
needle files, or by hammering with repeated blows on a
chasing or matting tool.
Once you have your design
ready, place the sterling disc
on the steel block and begin
hammering, as shown in
photo 1. (The steel block is
essential to this process
because it resists the hammer
blows. Otherwise, your metal
may become deformed, and
the stamp or chasing tool
won't do its job properly.)
When using commercial
stamps, I find that one blow
isn't enough to imprint the
metal. Use firm taps with the
chasing hammer, rocking the
stamp back and forth, and
up and down, to make sure
the whole design is imprint-
ed into the metal.

2. During chasing, the disc
may become slightly domed.
To reflatten the disc, turn it
over so the chasing faces
down, and hammer it lightly
with a wooden hammer or a
rawhide mallet. This type of
hammer is great for moving
and shaping metal without
leaving imprints on it.

3. Decide where on the back
of the disc you want the tubing—anywhere from the
middle to the top of the
bead. A circle template is
very useful in marking the
line for the position of the
tubing on the back of the
bead. Be sure your line is
consistent with the placement of the design on the
front of the disc, so that it
doesn't hang crookedly. To
find the length of tubing
you'll need, measure across
the disc at these points.

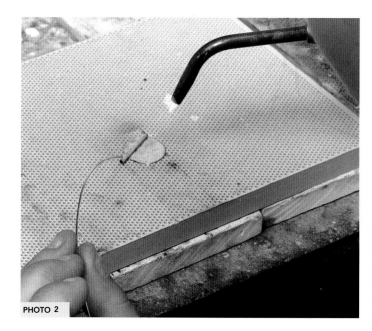

PHOTO 2

PHOTO 3

4. Saw the tubing 2 to 3 millimeters longer than the length you need. Flux the disc, then place the tubing on the line, with the extra length hanging over one edge.

5. Heat the piece until *all* the flux looks glassy, then place the solder on the overhanging tubing, as shown in photo 2. Continue to apply heat until the solder flows. The reason for placing the solder on the overhanging part of the tubing is to ensure that the solder runs right along the length of the tubing, keeping ugly solder blobs from getting on your disc. Pickle and rinse the piece.

6. Saw off the extra tubing. If the edges of the circle become deformed from chasing, use a bastard file to make the circle perfectly round again. When you do this, make sure to file *with* the circle, as shown in photo 3, not perpendicular to the metal's edge. Remove only the smallest amount of metal necessary. The more metal you remove, the easier it becomes to lose the perfect shape of the circle.

7. Sand the edges, and remove all the firescale from the back and front of the disc. Apply a final finish, as described on page 76. A patina can be especially nice on this bead, because the recessed imprints of the chasing tools remain black after the top surface of the disc has been sanded.

Twisted Wire & Tubing Beads

You can use plain or twisted wire to create vibrant bead designs around short lengths of silver tubing. Wire comes in many shapes, so you'll have plenty of opportunity to develop intricate shapes and patterns.

JOANNA GOLLBERG

MATERIALS & TOOLS

Sterling silver round wire,
18- to 24-gauge

Small tubing, 4 millimeters
or less outside diameter

Metal snips

Drill with a small drill bit
(see step 1)

Small mandrels, 1 to 5 mm
diameter

✖ **TECHNIQUES TO KNOW**
Cutting, Piercing & Sawing
Soldering
Finishing

✖ **DESIGNER'S NOTE:**
I often use sterling tubing,
in a limited range of sizes,
as mandrels when I'm bending wire into small circles
or curves.

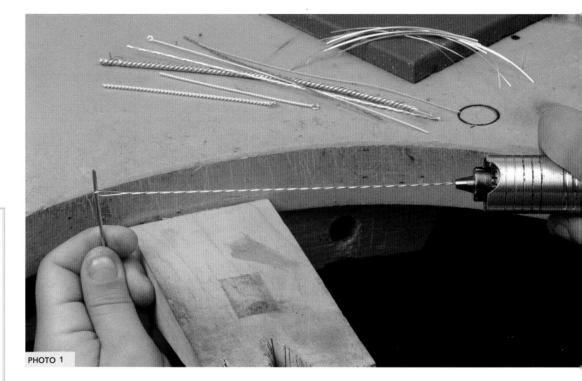

PHOTO 1

INSTRUCTIONS

1. Cut 36 to 48 inches (.9 to 1.2 m) of the round wire in any gauge you like. Bring the two ends together and insert them into the flex shaft chuck or into a handheld drill (either a manual augur or a cordless electric). I use the flex shaft for short lengths of twisted wire and the cordless for longer lengths. Insert a round mandrel into the doubled-over end of the wire, or hold it firmly with a pair of pliers, as shown in photo 1. Begin slowly twisting the wire.

The wire can be made into a very tight twist or can be kept at a loose twist. However, a loose twist often separates once it's formed into jump rings or other shapes, so I suggest making the twist fairly tight. Experiment with the tightness of the twist by winding the wire until it breaks. That will give you an idea of its limitations. If you want a very tight twist, which works well with the smaller-gauge wires, twist until the wire breaks, anneal the wire, then twist it again; for more information on annealing, see page 75. You can experiment by twisting wires of different gauges or shapes together, or by twisting more than two wires together.

2. Once you have the twisted wire ready, you're ready to design the bead. The wires can be manipulated into shapes or curls, or left as straight pieces. Use the jeweler's saw to cut the wire into workable lengths, then bend the lengths into the desired shapes over the mandrel. Remember to incorporate a short length of tubing into the design, for the string. When making several beads at once, I saw the needed number of tubing lengths and prepare all the beads for soldering at one time. You don't need to sand the tubing ends just yet; this can be done at the same time you sand the rest of the bead, after soldering it.

continued

Jump rings can make interesting geometric designs. Make a lot of jump rings at once by inserting a mandrel into the flex shaft, and put the wire in a slit of the chuck, as shown in photo 2. Twist the wire around the mandrel (see photo 3). Cut the long row into smaller rows, then saw the jump rings apart (see photo 4). You can make jump rings with plain wire or with twisted wire.

3. Place your bead on the soldering block, and flux all the joints. For a flat bead, you can use a single grade of solder, but for beads with a complex design where you'll join several pieces in separate soldering operations, start with hard solder, then use the medium and easy solder for later solderings.

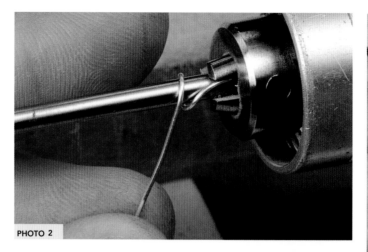

PHOTO 2

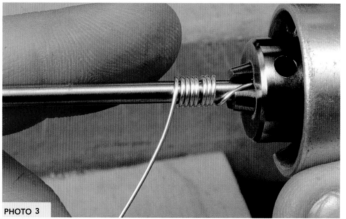

PHOTO 3

PHOTO 4

When soldering twisted wires, remember that the twisted wires will require more solder than does plain wire. The twist itself becomes another solder joint, so if you decide to solder using pallions instead of the stick method, be prepared with an extra amount of pallions already cut.

4. Pickle, rinse, and give the bead a final finish. At this time you can cut the tubing again if it seems too long, or just sand the ends to get rid of any burrs left from sawing. Be sure to sand any sharp points off your bead. Twisted wire looks lovely with a patina.

Domed Discs

This intriguing bead is shaped like a flying saucer. The two domed halves, embellished with organic and geometric openwork designs on one or both sides, are soldered together to make the unusual shape.

JOANNA GOLLBERG

MATERIALS & TOOLS

24-gauge sterling silver
discs, any diameter
Scribe
Center punch
Chasing hammer
Dapping block & daps
Drill, manual or electric,
with a small drill bit
Jeweler's saw and blade
Large bastard file
Barrette or triangular file

✖ **TECHNIQUES TO KNOW**
Cutting, Piercing & Sawing
Soldering
Finishing

✖ **DESIGNER'S NOTE:**
Sketch the design on paper,
shading in the negative spaces,
so you can be sure your design
is clear before you start cutting.
You can be creative about
where you decide to put the
bead holes; keep in mind that
there are two places they can
go—through the top of the
bead or through the side.

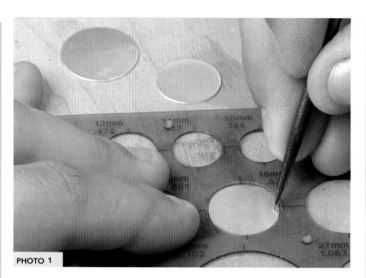

PHOTO 1

PHOTO 2

INSTRUCTIONS

1. Find the center of the disc, and scribe the X- and Y-axes on the disc, as shown in photo 1, to help you center your design. Draw the rest of your design on the disc. Make sure your scribe marks are deep enough that they won't disappear when you dap. You'll sand them off later.

2. Use a light tap of the chasing hammer on the end of the center punch, and make a small indention in each area that you want to saw out. These small indentations are your drill guide marks and will help keep the drill bit from whizzing around over the spot where you want to drill. It's essential that you make these marks before you dome the discs.

3. Choose a depression in your dapping block that the disc fits into. Put the disc into the depression with the design facedown. Using the chasing hammer and the dap of appropriate size (it should be a little smaller than the depression you're using), make firm taps on the end of the dap. Work first around the edge of the disc, then work toward the center, as shown in photo 2.

Dapping in this manner isn't absolutely necessary to make this particular bead, but it can be important in other techniques. The reason is that if you strike directly at the center of the disc, the metal will stretch thinner in the center than it does on the edges. For certain types of stone setting and other more advanced techniques, the thin metal in the center might ruin your plan. It's best to learn the correct method from the start.

4. Work the dap around the disc until it's completely recessed into the depression. If you want a higher dome on your bead, move the domed disc into successively smaller depressions on the block, only one size change at a time.

5. Sand or file the bottom edge until a nice rim appears (see photo 3). Be sure to move the file against the dome and not the dome against the file. Remember, the file cuts on the forward stroke only. Each half of the bead should rest perfectly flat on its rim, to make a strong joint later.

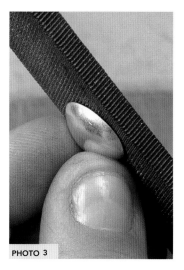

PHOTO 3

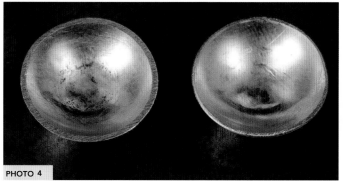

PHOTO 4

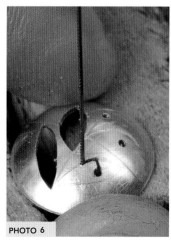

PHOTO 6

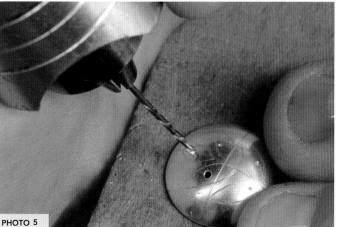

PHOTO 5

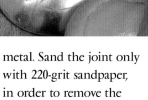

PHOTO 7

PHOTO 8

Photo 4 shows how the domes' edge looks before and after filing it. Test the rim's flatness by setting the dome on a steel block and looking at it at eye level.

6. Drill the holes for the piercing and sawing and for the bead hole, as shown in photo 5. Use a 3/0 blade for the sawing because the metal is fairly thin. Thread the blade through a drill hole and begin sawing just as you normally would on a flat sheet of metal (see photo 6). You'll find sawing a dome as easy as sawing on a flat sheet. When you're finished, use the needle files to remove any lines that look uneven.

7. Flux the rims of both domes, then put them together and place them on the soldering block. Again, you can use either the pallions or the stick soldering method, but I highly recommend that you stick solder

on this bead. There's less of a chance that the domes will shift when you stick solder than if you applied paillons to the bead with a solder pick.

8. Heat the metal and, when the flux looks glassy, deposit a small drop of solder right onto the joint, as shown in photo 7. Do this on at least two sides of the bead, making sure the solder has run completely around the joint. If any extra solder runs onto the surface of the bead, you can file it off later. Pickle and rinse the piece.

9. Using the bastard file, file around the joint until it appears to be one piece of

metal. Sand the joint only with 220-grit sandpaper, in order to remove the file marks.

10. Make the drill marks for the stringing holes by filing a mark with a triangular or square file, as shown in photo 8. Drill the holes on both sides of the bead, then sand them with 400-grit sandpaper.

11. Sand the entire bead with 400-grit sandpaper. Apply a final finish.

Variations

Solder two plain domes together, and sand the joint with 220-grit sandpaper, before sawing out shapes or designs from around the edge of the bead. Smooth out all surfaces and saw marks with 400-grit sandpaper, then apply a final finish using one of the methods described on page 76.

Appliquéd Hollow Forms

The process by which these appliquéd metal beads are made is deceptively simple. Once you understand how it's done, you can make your own hollow forms in any shape you can think of. The ingenious appliqué motif can even be made to look like enamelwork.

JOANNA GOLLBERG

PHOTO 1

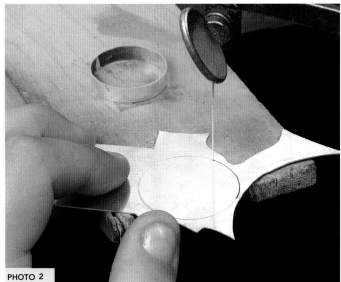

PHOTO 2

INSTRUCTIONS

✖ **DESIGNER'S NOTE:** This hollow bead is made in three sections: a circular top plate with the appliqué, a plain, circular bottom plate, and a center ring.

1. Cut a strip of metal for the center ring, and then join the ends. The height of this strip will determine the height of the bead. Decide on the diameter you'd like for your bead, and calculate the length of the strip by using the formula Circumference = Diameter x 3.14. For a bead 1 inch (2.5 cm) in diameter, cut a strip 3.14 inches (7.85 cm) in length.

2. Bring the ends of the strip together so they meet in a nice joint; don't worry about making a perfect circle. Solder them together, using hard solder. Pickle and rinse the metal.

3. Fit the ring onto a mandrel of appropriate size. Using a rawhide mallet or wooden hammer, gently hammer the ring into shape, as shown in photo 1. File, then sand the ring on both sides, so that it lies flat on the steel block.

4. Using the size of the center ring as your guide, saw out a circle for the bottom plate from the sheet of silver that is 3 to 5 millimeters larger in diameter than the ring, as shown in photo 2; it needn't be perfectly round. (This excess metal in the circle will absorb some of the torch's heat, so there is less chance of accidentally melting the piece during soldering.)

5. Flux the flat sheet metal, and place the ring on top of the circle. Heat the whole piece, but be sure to concentrate the

PHOTO 3

heat on the bottom circle of sheet metal. It would be very easy to inadvertently melt the ring, because the ring has a smaller volume of metal and will therefore heat faster than the flat circle. Next, apply medium solder (using the stick method or paillons) from the outside of the ring, and solder all the way around (see photo 3). The excess sheet metal and solder will be sawed off later. Pickle and rinse the piece.

PHOTO 4

PHOTO 5

PHOTO 6

6. Saw off the excess rim. You can file it smooth later. Trace the open side of the ring onto another piece of silver sheet, then saw out the shape.

7. Trace a third circle, making it 3 to 5 millimeters larger in diameter than the ring.

8. The smaller circle you cut in step 6 will be your appliqué piece. With the scribe, trace your design onto the smaller circle, as shown in photo 4, then pierce and saw out the negative spaces. Use a needle file to clean up any uneven saw lines.

9. Flux both circles. Place evenly spaced pallions of hard solder on the circle with the cutout design. It's important to use the minimum amount of solder necessary, or it will seep out and leave the excess in the negative spaces. Some experimentation will help. Melt the solder on the appliqué piece so that each paillon lies nearly flat on the sheet, as shown in photo 5. Pickle and rinse the piece, then reflux it.

10. Place the re-fluxed appliqué piece solder-side down onto the larger circle. Make sure you place it exactly in the center, with the same amount of excess rim all the way around. Begin heating the piece slowly, so that the flux doesn't bubble up too much and cause the appliqué to shift its position. Concentrate the heat on the bottom plate, because it will heat more slowly than the appliqué—simply because it's on the bottom. Once the bottom plate is hot enough for the solder to flow, pass your torch over the appliqué piece until it slowly sinks down, indicating that it has soldered. You'll also notice that a bright silver line of flowing solder will appear all the way around each piercing and sawing (see photo 6). Once the appliqué is soldered to the base plate, pickle and rinse the piece.

11. Flux the ring and the top plate. Set the ring on top of the appliquéd disc, with the appliqué side down, onto the soldering block. Make sure that the ring is centered on the disc. Solder, using easy solder.

Caution: Although it's possible to solder a hollow form without any air holes, there is a danger that some moisture from the pickling solution may have gotten trapped inside (through a hairline opening in a solder joint). When the form is reheated for more soldering operations, the moisture expands, and the piece may explode. If the pickled and rinsed piece is still hot, it's a good indication that the hollow form is full of moisture. For safety's sake, drill a pair of holes before proceeding with further soldering.

12. Saw off all excess metal, file, and sand with 220-grit sandpaper, making sure to remove all the firescale.

13. Mark the bead holes for drilling. Drill, then sand the piece to a smooth finish with 400-grit sandpaper. You can apply a final finish, or you can fill in the negative spaces with color using epoxy resin.

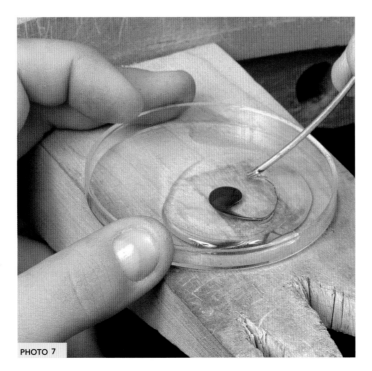

PHOTO 7

Variation

Epoxy resin is a sort of "plastic enamel" that you can use to add color or with which to embed small artifacts in your pieces. I use a nonyellowing two-part formula; this might be important if you want to embed tiny seeds or a picture in clear resin.

1. On a clean piece of scrap materials, mix equal parts of the epoxy resin. Stir it slowly with a toothpick or piece of scrap wire; try to avoid making too many bubbles. Add one or two drops of airbrush pigment, then stir slowly until the pigment is completely mixed with the epoxy resin, as shown in photo 7.

2. Transfer the mixture into the open spaces of your appliqué, until the cavities are full. Put one or two extra drops of the epoxy resin into the open spaces to make sure they're completely filled.

3. Adjust the flame to a smaller size. To bring all the air bubbles to the surface, pass the flame over the epoxy. Let the epoxy dry overnight, until it's almost rock hard. If it's at all soft, you probably didn't mix the epoxy in exactly equal parts, or there's too much pigment in the mixture. If necessary, you can peel the soft mixture out of the cavity quite easily, or use your scribe to dig it out, before trying again.

4. File off any excess epoxy with the bastard file, then sand it with 400-grit sandpaper. Use one of the finishing techniques to give the bead the kind of surface you'd like, then wash it with a grease-removing dishwashing soap to remove any grime that might be sticking to the epoxy from the finishing process.

Hollow Forms with Filigree

Delicate filigree designs have an ancient history, and their enduring appeal is quite easy to achieve. Building on your experience with some of the previous projects, you'll find the hollow forms a perfect canvas for your own filigree creations.

JOANNA GOLLBERG

MATERIALS & TOOLS

Sterling silver sheet, 26- or 24-gauge
Sterling or fine silver wire, 18- to 24-gauge
Jeweler's saw and blade
Large round mandrel or dap
Wooden hammer or rawhide mallet; optional
Large bastard file
Cross-locking tweezers
Drill, manual or electric, with a small drill bit
Small embroidery scissors
Compressed charcoal block

✖ **TECHNIQUES TO KNOW**

Cutting, Piercing & Sawing
Soldering
Finishing

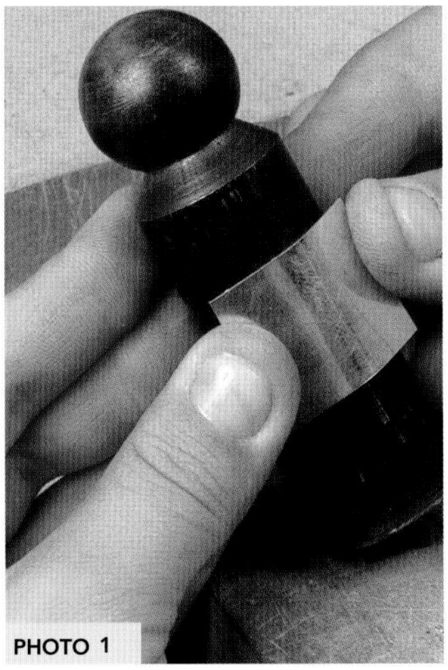

PHOTO 1

INSTRUCTIONS

✖ **DESIGNER'S NOTE:**
Although it looks complex, this bead is made with just five parts: a curved piece of metal, a flat base plate, two sides or end caps, and the wire decoration itself.

1. Saw a rectangle from a sheet of 24- or 26-gauge sterling silver. A $^{3}/_{4}$ x $1^{1}/_{4}$ inch (20 x 30 mm) rectangle is a nice size to start with.

2. Bend the rectangle around a large mandrel of some kind (I used the daps from my dapping set), so that it makes a curved arch, as shown in photo 1. You can bend it with your hands or a hammer or mallet. File or sand the edges of the arch so they're flat and even, and lay them on a steel block to check them.

3. Using the curved piece as a size guide, saw out a slightly larger bottom plate. The extra metal will be sawed off later.

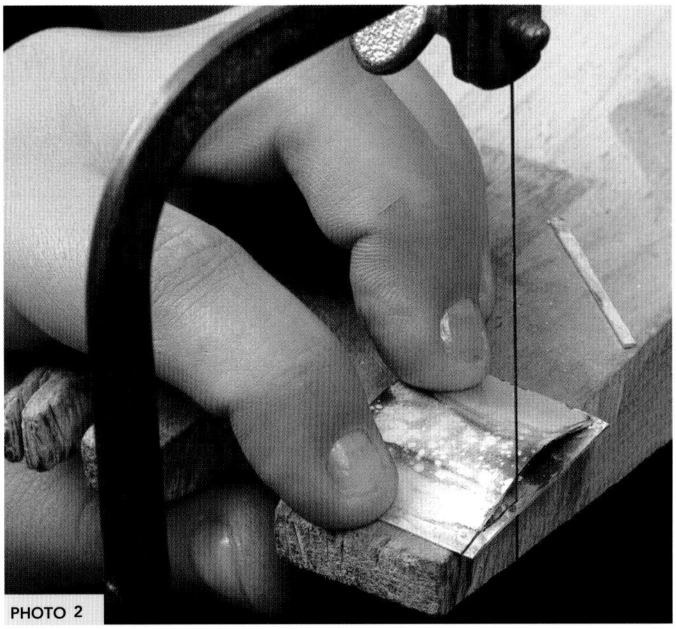

PHOTO 2

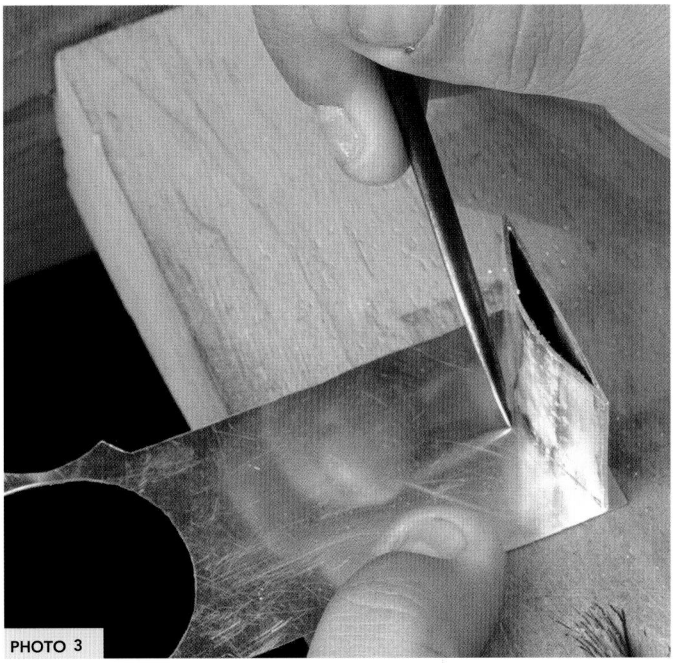

PHOTO 3

4. Solder the curved piece of metal onto the base plate with hard solder. Heat the whole piece, but concentrate the heat on the bottom sheet of metal. Because the bottom sheet lies on top of the soldering block, it's able to absorb more heat than the curved piece can. Pickle and rinse the piece.

5. Saw off the extra metal. Be sure to hold the saw frame at a 90-degree angle to the base plate, as shown in photo 2. This will help ensure that the end caps will be at a 90-degree angle to the base plate. File the open ends with the bastard file.

6. Use the open end of the soldered form to trace two end cap pieces, slightly larger than the openings they'll cover, from the sterling (see photo 3 on page 95). The extra metal will absorb some of the torch's heat, so there is less chance of accidentally melting the piece during soldering.

7. Apply flux to the end caps and, using medium solder, flood the surfaces with solder. Apply flux to the open spaces on both ends of your bead. Use a pair of wooden handled cross-locking tweezers to hold the bead while you solder on one end cap (see photo 4). Flip the bead over and solder on the other end cap. I find this method much easier and quicker than trying to set up the whole piece so that it won't fall over during the soldering. Pickle the piece, then rinse it.

8. Saw off all the extra metal, then file the edges with a bastard file. Sand first with 220-, then 400-grit sandpaper.

9. Determine the placement of the bead holes, then mark and drill them into the end caps; be sure to review the cautionary note, on page 92, about soldering a closed hollow form.

PHOTO 4

10. Make twisted wire, as explained for the Twisted-Wire & Tubing Bead on page 85. I like to have several different styles of twisted wire on hand when I'm developing the design. You can twist the wire into any shape you want; follow popular filigree wire forms, or make up your own. Try using plain round wire mixed in with the twisted wire for a beautiful effect.

11. Make the balls from fine silver. I prefer fine silver rather than sterling because it seems to make rounder balls, but you can use sterling silver if you prefer. This is easy and relaxing work. Using 24-gauge silver wire, follow the instructions from step 2, on page 86, to make a lot of small jump rings. Snip them apart with a pair of embroidery scissors. Using jump rings ensures that each circle of metal makes the same size ball.

PHOTO 5

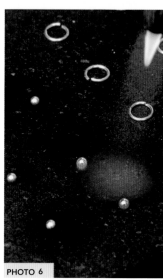
PHOTO 6

12. On a compressed-charcoal block, line up the jump rings in rows, leaving a bit of space between them so they don't stick together when melted. Reduce the size of the torch's flame, and melt the balls, as shown in photos 5 and 6. I always make a lot of balls at once, because they roll off my worktable and get lost, or I end up using more in my design than I'd originally planned. Some gardening suppliers have seed canisters with clear glass lids that are wonderful for keeping balls and wire parts organized; film canisters or egg cartons work well, too.

13. Make a "glue" from flux that will make the pieces stick to the curved surface of your bead before soldering. Mix a very small amount of liquid or paste flux with water (the solution should remain quite watery), and dip each wire and ball into the mixture before placing the pieces on the bead. This way, the entire design is in place with some of the flux already applied, and the tiny pieces won't jump around during the soldering. Let the pieces dipped in the flux glue dry completely. (If the pieces move after all, you may have used too much flux in the glue mixture, or the flux isn't dry enough.) The amount of flux in the glue isn't enough to allow the solder to flow, so I use a no-hands method to apply more flux once the piece is heated. Make some powdered flux that you can sift onto your already heated piece. Using this dry flux method helps to create an even temperature on the surface of your bead, and it makes multiple soldering jobs quite easy to do in one step. It's been a blessing for me when making jewelry, and I highly recommend you make some for yourself.

PHOTO 7

Empty a jar of paste flux into a casserole dish or onto some aluminum foil, and set it in the sun to dry. Put the dried flux in a fine mortar and pestle, and grind it as finely as you can. You can then put this dry flux into a salt shaker or—even better—fabricate a metal container of your own to house the flux.

14. Begin heating the bead with your torch. Once the entire surface is slightly hot, sift some dry flux onto the bead, making sure to cover all the wires and balls, as shown in photo 7. Heat the bead some more and, using easy solder, stick-solder all the decorative wires in one soldering step. You can use pallions, but the work will be more labor-intensive and difficult. You might prefer to solder the wires first, then pickle and rinse the piece before refluxing and soldering the balls; it's up to you. Pickle and rinse a final time.

15. Sand the bead again with 400-grit sandpaper, making sure to remove all the firescale. Finish with any technique you desire; I find the bristle sanding discs work wonderfully for finishing filigree.

JOANNA GOLLBERG

Marriage of Metals Necklace, 2001. Center: 1¾ x 3 in. (4.4 x 7.6 cm); left & right: ½ x 3 in. (1.3 x 7.6 cm). Photo by Seth Tice-Lewis

I began making jewelry in 1992 when I took a class on enameling and basic jewelry making at Penland School of Crafts. During my two-week stint there, I realized that never had time passed for me in a nicer way, and I was hooked on making jewelry. After graduating from Warren Wilson College in 1995, I attended the Fashion Institute of Technology in New York City, where I spent two more years studying jewelry techniques and design, earning an associate of applied science degree in 1997. I then returned to Asheville, North Carolina— my hometown—where I worked driving a catering van for one long year. I made jewelry on the side, and as soon as the first gallery bought a significant amount of jewelry from me, I quit the catering company and went into business for myself, full time.

I've been selling my production line of marriage-of-metal jewelry for more than four years. I teach jewelry part time at two local colleges and sell my work at craft fairs on the East Coast. I'm a member of both the Southern Highland Handicraft Guild and the Piedmont Craftsmen. I'm

Marriage of Metals & Black Freshwater Pearls Necklace, 2001. Pendant: 2 x 3 in. (5 x 7.6 cm). Photo by Seth Tice-Lewis

Marriage of Metals Pendant & Earrings, 2001. Pendant: 1¾ in. (4.4 cm) diameter; earrings: ⅝ x ¾ in. (1.6 x 1.9 cm). Photo by Seth Tice-Lewis

very lucky to be involved in an active artist community in Asheville, and I do my best to attend the monthly meetings of a group of jewelers, the Mountain Metalsmiths, which I helped create. Making jewelry is one of the most satisfying and fun things I've ever done, and I consider myself lucky to be able to have my passion as my job. I look forward to a lifetime of learning and sharing my knowledge with others in the field of metal-smithing.

Metal GALLERY

Color Play (detail), Kristen Frantzen Orr, 2001. Largest: ¾ in. (1.9 cm). Photo by David Orr

Roundel Overlay Beads, Timothy A. Hansen, 1998. Large: 1¼ x ¹³⁄₁₆ x 1¼ in. (3.1 x 2.1 x 3.1 cm); medium: ¹¹⁄₁₆ x ¾ x ¹¹⁄₁₆ in. (1.7 x 1.9 x 1.7 cm); small: ⅞ x ⅝ x ⅞ in. (2.2 x 1.6 x 2.2 cm). Photo by artist

Adjustable Orbital Model #1, Susie Ganch, 1997. 2 x 12¼ x 12¼ in. (5 x 31.1 x 31.1 cm). Photo by Jim Wildeman

Mokume Beads (three in a series), Timothy A. Hansen, 1998. Large: ¾ x ¹⁵⁄₁₆ x ¾ in. (1.9 x 2.4 x 1.9 cm); small: ¹¹⁄₁₆ x ⅞ x ¹¹⁄₁₆ in. (1.7 x 2.2 x 1.7 cm). Photo by artist

Copper Drum Beads, Fae Mellichamp, 2000. ⁹⁄₁₆ x ⁷⁄₁₆ x ⁷⁄₁₆ in. (1.4 x 1.1 x 1.1 cm). Photo by Robert Overton

Saturn Bead (one in a series), Timothy A. Hansen, 1998. ¾ x 1¼ x 11/4 in. (1.9 x 3.1 x 3.1 cm). Photo by artist

Lavendar Green, Kristen Frantzen Orr, 2000. Largest: ⅞ in. (2.2 cm). Photo by Ralph Rippe

RetroFlex, Susie Ganch, 1996. From ¾ in. (1.9 cm) to ½ in. (3.8 cm). Photo by Jim Wildeman

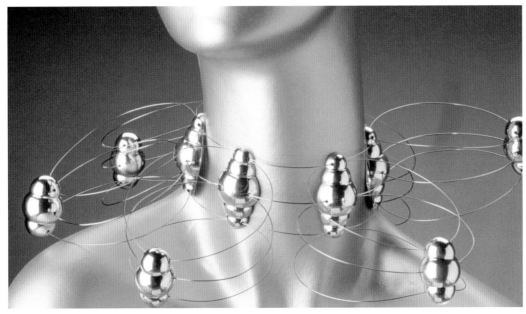

Adjustable Orbital Model #2, Susie Ganch, 1997. 4 x 12 x 12 in. (10.2 x 30.5 x 30.5 cm).
Photo by Jim Wildeman

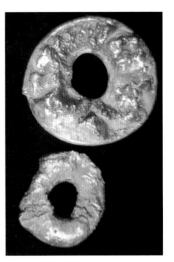

Bronze Beads, Ernest P. Neri, 2001. From 1 in. (2.5 cm) to ½ in. (1.3 cm). Photo by artist

Red Bead Slider, Pat Moses-Caudel, 2001. 2 x 2½ in. (5 x 6.4 cm). Photo by Amanda Caudel

Copper Drum Beads, Fae Mellichamp, 2000. 9/16 x 7/16 x 7/16 in. (1.4 x 1.1 x 1.1 cm). Photo by Robert Overton

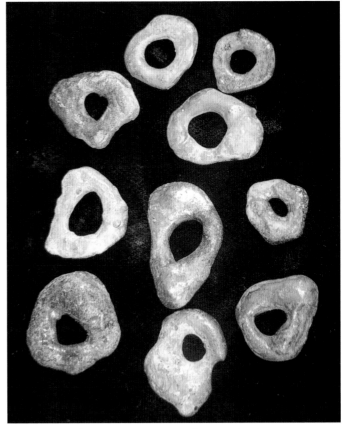

Assorted Beads, Ernest P. Neri, 2001. ½ in. (1.3 cm). Photo by artist

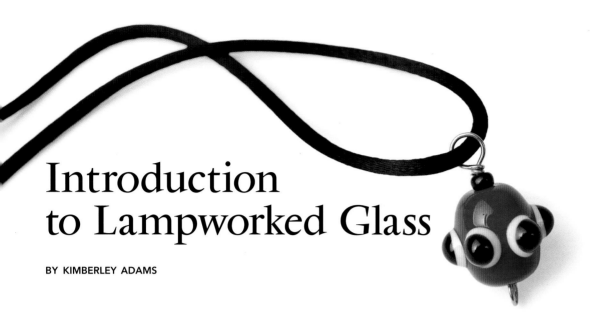

Introduction to Lampworked Glass

BY KIMBERLEY ADAMS

Lampworking glass (shaping glass in the molten state over a torch) is a wonderful and fascinating way to make beads. Glass, especially in its molten state, is an amazing medium. Once you know some essentials about glass and have an understanding of how to use the torch, you're ready to master a few basic skills. Then the rest is up to your imagination! You'll soon be designing beads in your sleep!

The Basics

The essential information you need to know in order to get started begins here, from how to light the torch to winding a basic round bead.

Getting the Right Glass

The soft glass rods used in these projects take little time to heat and bring to molten in the flame. This Italian glass also has a wonderful palette available. Rods are easy to use because they roll nicely in the hand. While hard glass stays quite stiff in the molten state, molten soft glass is easier to manipulate, shape, push, and pull when you're making beads. You'll find the glass rods you need wherever supplies for stained glass are sold.

Glass is a mixture of sand, potash, and lime. There are many formulas and characteristics of glass, and these are categorized by the rate at which the glass expands and contracts as it's heated and cooled. The number that expresses this is called the coefficient of expansion (COE). In order for different glasses to be used together in one bead, their COEs must be compatible, within a few points of each other.

The COE indicates how much heat is needed to soften the glass to a moldable, molten state. You'll use a soft glass; be sure to get rods with a COE of 104. Hard glass, such as borosilicate (oven-safe glassware), has a relatively low COE of 32, and it takes a lot of heat to get to the molten state.

Lampworking glass rods come in a rainbow of colors.

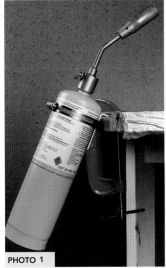
PHOTO 1

Torches

There are two basic fuel sources available for bead making. You may want to start by using brazing fuel while you're getting used to working with molten, moving glass; photo 1 shows the basic setup. (Brazing fuel is a propane modified to burn hotter than regular propane.) Only one design of torch, known by the brand name Hot Head (see photo 2), works with brazing fuel. The specially designed torch head draws in a lot of air, and this helps keep the glass from burning in the flame.

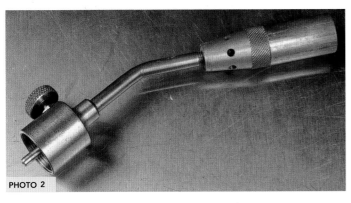
PHOTO 2

There are many types of torches available that burn a combination of oxygen and propane. They produce a much hotter flame than brazing fuel and will heat the glass to molten faster. While the oxygen/propane takes some getting used to, this mix allows you greater flexibility in the size and detail of your beads. Either setup will work with the soft glass used for the projects in this book.

BRAZING FUEL SETUP

Brazing fuel can be purchased in small 1-pound (.45 kg) nonrefillable tanks. The torch head attaches directly to the top of the tank; screw it on tightly. Use a hose clamp that fits around the tank to fasten an L-bracket near the top. Use a C-clamp to fasten the other part of the L-bracket to the tabletop. Be sure the torch is facing forward (that is, away from you). You may want to angle the torch further forward by bending the L-bracket so the flame is positioned at an angle, as it is

in photo 1; you can adjust this after you light the torch for the first time.

Brazing fuel is also available in larger, refillable tanks. One end of the hose secures directly to the tank, and the other end connects to the torch head with a special fitting. If you do use brazing fuel, have your fuel supplier assist with the correct hose attachments. Take the Hot Head torch with you, so the supplier gives you the correct hose and fitting. Once you're home, secure a small hose clamp and bracket around the fitting, and use a C-clamp to secure the other end of the L-bracket to the tabletop, as with the 1-pound (.45 kg) tank.

LIGHTING PROCEDURES

Lighting a brazing fuel torch is fairly simple. Try lighting the torch a few times in order to get used to the process. (For a large tank, you'll open the valve on the top of the tank about three-quarters of a full turn. This allows the tank to be turned off quickly in case of an emergency.) For either size of brazing fuel tank, get the feel of turning the torch's valve counterclockwise, letting out a slow flow of gas—you'll hear a low rushing sound—then turn the flow off. Get the striker ready, and slowly open the torch valve again. Depress the striker's trigger (see photo 3), right

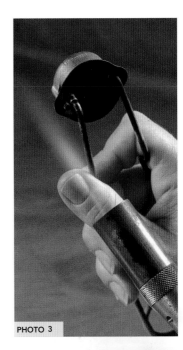
PHOTO 3

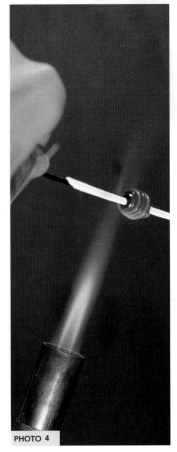
PHOTO 4

over the top of the torch; this might take a few tries to ignite the fuel. Once it's lit, turn up the gas so the flame has a sharp blue cone, 1 inch (2.5 cm) in length, extending from the tip of the torch (see photo 4 on page 103). The torch makes a rushing noise while it's lit. If you have trouble using a striker, try lighting the torch with a match held just under the rim at the end of the torch.

For all types of fuel (except the 1-pound [.45 kg] size), perform a leak test. Spray a weak mixture of Ivory dishwashing liquid and water (only a soap without a petroleum base, such as Ivory brand soap, may be used to test oxygen; others may spontaneously combust!) on all the connections for both oxygen and propane. If bubbles appear around these connections, tighten

it down and spray again. Propane and brazing fuels have a marker odor added to them so you'll know if they're leaking, but oxygen has no odor, so test it carefully each time you change the connections. In any case, be sure to have a professional help you set up an oxygen-assisted torch.

Lampworking tools (clockwise from top left): quenching bowl, powdered bead release, clear protective lenses, didymium lenses, nippers, mandrels, vermiculite, glass rods on rod rest, pliers, flat tweezers, bead rake, graphite paddle on grooved marver, bead reamers

Workbench & Tools

It's important that you work in a clean and safe environment with good ventilation. Ideally, you should install an overhead exhaust hood that will draw stale air and dust outside, away from you, and through a duct. At the minimum, have some cross-ventilation that won't interrupt the flow of the flame (i.e., air should flow from behind you). The room should be bare, with no carpeting, books, paper, curtains, or other flammable items. Install a fire extinguisher, and make sure the exit is easily accessed.

Any sturdy table can be used as long as the entire top is protected with a heat-proof material, such as galvanized steel or heat-proof board. A tall table allows you to work while standing or sitting at a tall stool; sometimes standing is a good rest for the back if you've been working for a long time.

A *marver* is a flat, heatproof surface that can be used to roll the molten glass into different bead shapes. Marvers are made of graphite, steel, aluminum, or other heatproof material, and special ones have patterns on them so you can put interesting textures on the glass surface.

Use tweezers and pliers to pick up decorative elements (bits of glass, metal leaf) and place them on the hot bead. Both the pointed and flat-nosed versions are useful. Bent nose pliers let you grasp a bit of molten glass (to make a stringer), yet let your hand and arm remain in a comfortable working position.

A graphite paddle is used to shape the molten bead. Graphite works very well because it doesn't take as much heat out of the glass as a metal paddle would. Graphite is also slippery, making it easier to roll the bead on.

A rod rest is a bent strip of metal with notches cut into the bend, and is used to set a hot rod on when you're done with it at the torch. With the tip of the rod in the air it will cool better, and there's less of a possibility that it will crack. It also helps keep all the hot glass in one central location. Hot glass is wound around a steel rod, or mandrel. During the bead making process, the mandrel holds the hot bead. Once they've cooled, you can separate the bead from the mandrel. Mandrels can be purchased from lampworking suppliers. They're available in various diameters; 3/32 inch (2.4 mm) was used for all the projects shown in this book. Mandrels can be purchased in 9- and 12-inch (22.9 and 30.5 cm) lengths.

Bead release is similar to a potter's kiln wash. This material provides a thin barrier layer between the glass bead and the steel mandrel, and allows the bead to separate from the rod after it cools. Bead release is available premixed, or you can mix the powder with water to a pancake-batter consistency. Dip the mandrel into the release for an even, thin coating that covers about 2½ inches (6.4 cm) of one end of the mandrel. Allow it to air dry in an upright position, or dry it in the flame if the brand you use allows it.

A quenching bowl—a small dish with water—is good to have at the table so that tools can be cooled between uses; otherwise, it's possible that the tools might get hot enough to stick to the glass.

A bead rake is a hooked mandrel or dental tool used to push and pull designs on the surface of the bead. These can be purchased from a bead supplier, or you can make one from a bent mandrel that's been filed to a point.

Use a striker as the flame source for lighting a torch; these are commonly used to light an outdoor cooking grill. Lighting the torch this way takes a little practice, but it's safer than having an extra fuel source, like a cigarette lighter, at your bench. Matches can also be used until you're more comfortable using the striker.

The projects in this book are cooled without the use of a kiln. Instead, an electric slow cooker filled with vermiculite works very well for smaller beads. In order to avoid inhaling the dust from vermiculite, pour it into the cooker outdoors, with the wind blowing away from you. The vermiculite may have an odor when it's first heated, so be sure to have plenty of ventilation at that time.

A diamond file or bead reamer is used to clean out the hole of the bead after it's taken off the mandrel. If the release is soft enough, pipe cleaners will also do the job.

Eye protection is extremely important and must be used. The most common protective glasses for lampworking use *didymium lenses*. The possibility of glass popping off the end of a rod that's heated too quickly, and the presence of a soda flare from the glass in the flame, requires a lens that both protects your eyes and filters the light. The soda flare will be brighter with an oxygen/propane flame than with other fuels, and might otherwise keep you from seeing what you are doing in the flame. If you're using a brazing fuel, you must nevertheless use some type of protective lenses, even though the soda flare won't be as bright.

• Some carbon monoxide is created by the burning flame, so good ventilation is very important.

• Avoid inhaling dust from bead release, powdered glass, and from vermiculite. Provide good ventilation and wipe down dusty surfaces with a damp towel to help minimize the potentially irritating and harmful dust.

• Remember that hot glass looks just like cold glass! There are a few colors that change appearance in the flame, but even when the hot part of the rod or bead has returned to the original color it's still hot enough to burn. Keep all recently heated rods on the rod rest. Keep a bowl of water and a burn cream or aloe plant close by. Keep long hair tied back, and wear nonpoly-ester clothing that covers as much skin as possible. Avoid open-neck shirts and loose sleeves.

• Never leave the burning torch unattended. Remember that the torch head will stay hot for quite a while after the flame is off.

• Keep a working fire extinguisher within easy reach.

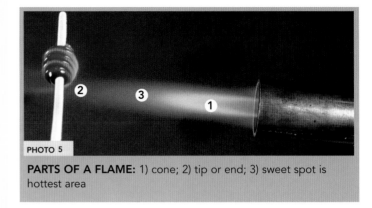

PHOTO 5

PARTS OF A FLAME: 1) cone; 2) tip or end; 3) sweet spot is hottest area

Basic Techniques

The change from cold to molten glass appears to be a magical process, but practicing the techniques described here will help you gain control over the basic lampworking method.

Heating & Melting Glass over Flame

The body of your torch's flame has several different temperatures. It's important that you use the correct part of the flame during various stages of the lampworking process. Try to become familiar with photo 5, which shows the parts of a brazing fuel flame, so you can control the molten glass. The flame produced by other types of fuels will look somewhat different; check with a reference source if you use another fuel.

In order to avoid thermal shock, the glass must be heated very slowly. Thermal shock can cause the glass to pop off the end of the rod. Not only is this frightening, but bits of glass may hit you—and the glass can be hot enough to burn! (That's another reason why protective lenses are required.)

1. Hold the glass rod in your dominant hand (like a pencil), and keep it angled down a bit, as if you were writing with it. Put the tip into the back or end of the flame, where the blue has almost disappeared (see photo 6). Roll the rod back and forth between your fingers, so that the entire circumference of the rod—not just one side—is heated. You'll begin to see a bit of a glow at the end of the rod as it heats, even through your didymium lenses. This is the sign that you can now

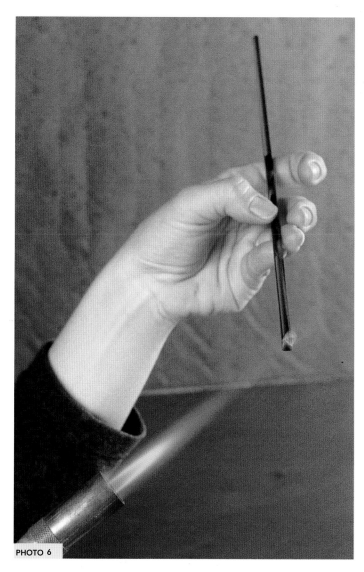

PHOTO 6

PHOTO 7

PHOTO 8

begin moving the rod closer into the flame. As you keep turning the rod, gradually bring it to within 2 inches (5 cm) of the cone (or circle of cones, for an oxygen/propane fuel) in the flame (see photo 7). This is often called the sweet spot. Heat a $^{1}/_{2}$- to $^{5}/_{8}$-inch (1.3 to 1.6 cm) section of glass.

2. As the rod heats, it begins to soften and slump; now change the angle of the rod to a horizontal position, as shown in photo 8. Remember to continue rolling the rod in your fingers, to keep the softened glass centered. If it droops too much, the glass is hard to control. You're trying to stay ahead of the force of gravity that will pull the softened glass down; this gets easier with practice.

Winding a Basic Round Bead

Once you've learned how to get the glass to the molten stage, you're ready to learn how to wind the hot glass around the mandrel and make a bead.

108

1. Hold the glass rod in your hand like a pencil, as before. Hold the mandrel horizontally in your other hand with an overhand method, held in your curled fingers, and balanced with the little finger, as shown in photos 9 and 10; you'll turn it with your thumb and index finger. The mandrel must also be heated, so the glass will stick to it. Put the mandrel at the end of the flame, behind the glass rod, and heat it until it just begins to glow; keep turning it.

2. As the tip of the glass rod reaches the molten state, bring the cool end of the rod around, so that it's pointed toward you. Bring the glass rod and mandrel together at a 90-degree angle, as shown in photo 11.

3. Reaching through the flame with the glass rod and with the mandrel slightly below the flame, lightly touch the tip of the mandrel with the molten end of the glass (see photo 12).

4. Slowly turn the mandrel away from you, pulling the molten glass over the top of

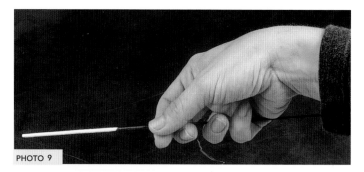
PHOTO 9

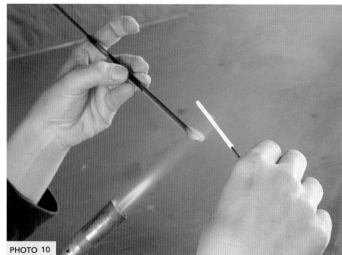
PHOTO 10

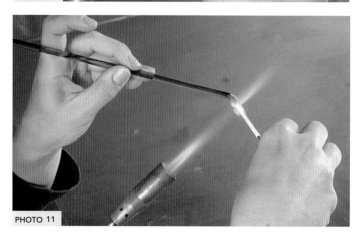
PHOTO 11

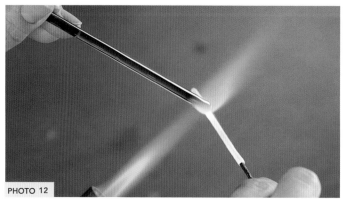
PHOTO 12

the mandrel (see photo 13). Try not to move the rod up or down the mandrel; hold it in one place, wrapping the glass on top of itself as you wind it onto the mandrel, until the section of molten glass has been pulled off the end of the glass rod.

5. Lift the glass rod slightly so that the bead and rod are $1/2$ inch (1.3 cm) apart; they will still be connected. Put these still-connected sections of glass into the flame, letting the flame separate them from each other (the molten glass only separates cleanly if it's done in the flame). Don't be tempted to pull the glass rod away from the bead quickly, before the two sections are completely separated, or you'll have a very thin "hair" of glass.

6. Once the bead and rod are separated, put the rod in the rest, with the hot end supported by the rod rest. Keep turning the bead in the flame, rolling the mandrel in both directions, to keep the entire bead evenly heated.

7. Bring the bead out of the flame while still turning it. If the bead isn't symmetrical, hold it with the heavy side up for a brief one- or two-second pause, letting gravity even up the volume of glass. This will happen quickly if the glass is very molten.

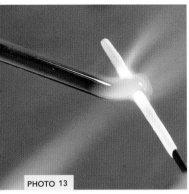

PHOTO 13

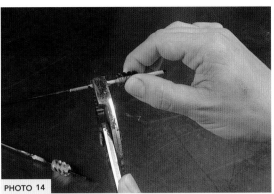

PHOTO 14

PHOTO 15

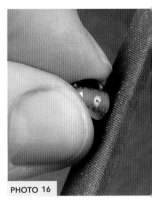

PHOTO 16

8. When the bead is symmetrical, cool it by moving it out to the end of the flame. This way, the bead stays warm, but the glass begins to return to the rigid state. Continue turning the mandrel.

9. Flame annealing is a process of gradual cooling that carefully controls the stress on the glass through successive temperature ranges at a slowed, controlled rate. If you're serious about making lampworked beads, consider purchasing a small electric kiln. The entire cooling process—from 975° F (523° C) to room temperature—takes three to four hours, depending on the size of the beads. Cooling beads in an electric slow cooker filled with vermiculite is acceptable for small rounded beads, but it doesn't work well for flattened ones that have a thinner place over the mandrel. This book demonstrates how to make beads that can be cooled with the slow cooker method.

• If you're using a brazing fuel torch, move the bead

(turning the mandrel as before) in and out of the flame, eventually keeping the bead out of the flame more than it's in it, until the glow disappears.

• To begin flame annealing with an oxygen/propane torch, slowly turn off the the oxygen with the side knob. Keep the bead in the orange-red propane flame for one minute, turning it as it cools and returns to the rigid state, until the glow disappears.

10. Put away the bead in the vermiculite-filled, heated cooker for 45 minutes, then move it into a container of room-temperature vermiculite. Take care, when adding more beads, that they don't touch each other.

11. Keep the beads in this container until they reach room temperature. The length of time this takes depends on how many beads are in the container, the size of the beads, and the size of the container.

Removing the Cooled Bead from the Mandrel

1. After the beads cool to room temperature, they're ready to be removed from the mandrel. First, soak the beads in cool water for a few minutes, to soften the bead release material a bit and to contain any dust. The bead release will be stiff but crumbly.

2. Hold the mandrel with pliers, close to the bead, then grasp the bead firmly in your hand and turn it, as shown in photo 14, breaking the tension between the bead and the bead release. You may need to use a paper towel or a rubber jar lid gripper to help you hold and turn the bead. Try not to bend the mandrel, or your next bead will get stuck on it.

3. Use the bead file or a reamer to scrape the release out of the bead's hole. You may have to scrape it and rinse it in water a few times, to get out all the residue, because a clean hole is important. The hole will always have a rough, etched look on that inside surface.

4. If the ends of the beads have any sharp places (see photo 15), file these points with a flat fine file, as shown in photo16. It's important to file away sharp places that might cut through a string or cord.

Now that the basics of laying molten glass onto a mandrel have been covered, we'll add to that process. You should review these basic techniques for heating glass and winding a basic bead until you're familiar with them.

Making Beautiful Beads

109

Sputnik Beads

This bead, with its Space Age look, is a fun way to build on the basic round bead technique you just learned.

KIMBERLEY ADAMS

Kimberley Adams

INSTRUCTIONS

✳ DESIGNER'S NOTE: For this project, you'll learn how to build up the hot glass for a nice round bead that is larger than the basic one you learned to make. For that one, the amount of glass used was approximately the width of the glass rod itself. This bead should measure approximately twice the width of the glass rod.

1. Start by winding a round bead about the size of a small grape. As you bring the glass to the molten state and wrap it around the mandrel, build up a bit more glass for a larger bead.

2. While the rod and mandrel are in the flame, separate them; lay the rod onto the rod rest, and allow the bead to soften and get round.

3. Once the bead is round, let it cool a bit by moving it to the back of the flame. Most of the glow should go out of the bead, but don't let it cool too much. Keep the bead in the back flame, or lift the bead in and out of the flame slowly, always turning it.

4. Put the first dot color into the flame, bringing only a small pea-sized portion of the rod to molten. Just to one side and out of the flame, touch the glass rod to the bead, coming straight up

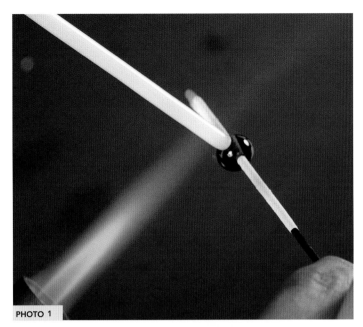

PHOTO 1

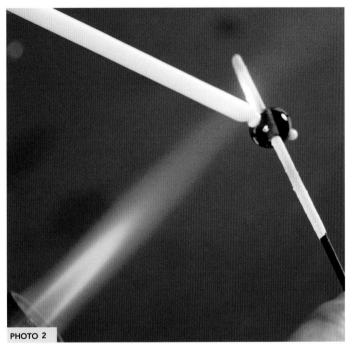

PHOTO 2

from the surface of the bead, as shown in photo 1. Lift the rod, moving that still-connected area into the flame, separating the rod from the bead and leaving a small amount of glass behind. The amount of pressure you use and the amount of glass you've heated will affect how much glass is left behind on the bead.

5. Heat a small bit of glass again and set another dot of color onto the bead (see photo 2). Repeat as desired, laying dots evenly around the bead. Try to heat the same amount of glass each time so that all the dots will be the same size. Whenever you're heating a bit more of the dot color, move the bead into the back flame, always turning it, so that it doesn't cool too much.

6. The dots may be a bit pointy. If so, bring the bead into the hotter part of the flame, turning it constantly. This heats the dots so they'll soften and round off. Once they're rounded, move the bead to the cooler part of the flame again.

7. Now add a second color by heating a rod and setting down a smaller amount of glass on top of each of the first round of dots. Try adding still more colors, each time setting down smaller and smaller amounts of glass.

8. Once you have all the dots rounded off and your bead is evenly heated and glowing, begin flame annealing the bead. Turn off the oxygen (if you're using an oxygen/propane torch) and continue to turn the bead as it cools, until the glow is gone. Put the bead away in vermiculite.

Groovy Beads

These grooved and groovy beads show the fluid qualities inherent in glass. Again, you'll build on techniques learned earlier. Take a look at metal tools on your tool bench, or use a slotted metal kitchen spoon for interesting patterns!

KIMBERLEY ADAMS

INSTRUCTIONS

DESIGNER'S NOTE:

A graphite paddle and a special grooved marver are used to shape this bead, so keep them nearby. Practice is essential, but well worth it, because these tools add many options for shaping, rather than the glass always acting like a liquid and creating only round forms as a result.

Place the grooved side of the marver at the edge of the table near your dominant hand. When the marver is close to the edge, you can more easily hold the mandrel parallel to the surface of the marver.

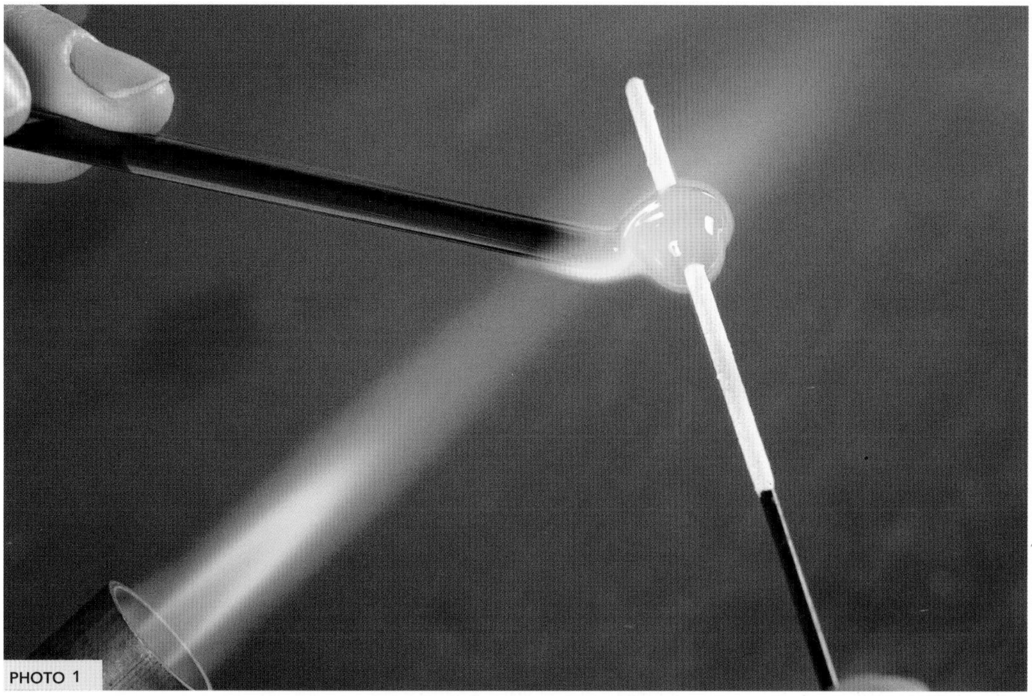

PHOTO 1

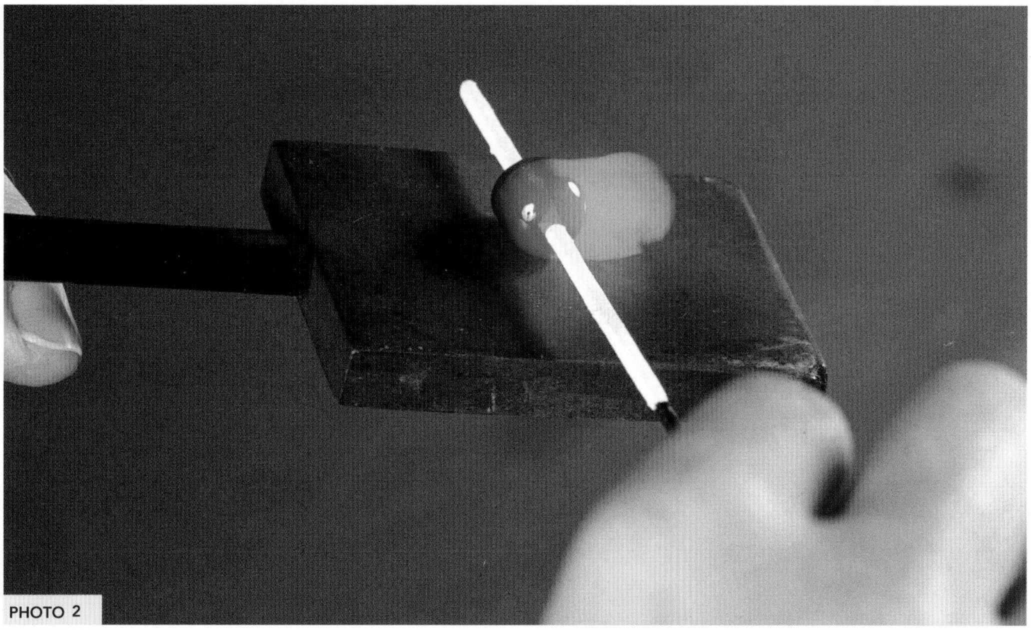

PHOTO 2

1. This time you'll add glass along a wider section of the mandrel—about three times the width of the glass rod (see photo 1). This bead will also have a larger diameter than the first one you made. Heat the glass rod and wind an oval-shaped bead slightly larger than the previous project; the bead should be nicely molten and quite symmetrical.

2. Bring the bead out of the flame. Pick up the graphite paddle in your nondominant hand. Hold the paddle at eye level so you can see that you're rolling the bead with the mandrel parallel to the paddle, as shown in photo 2.

3. Roll the bead back and forth a few times. Start with a very light touch and increase the pressure, a little at a time, as the glass cools and firms up, reshaping the glass to be like a tube or barrel with straight sides. If the glass cools before you have the shape you want, reheat it to just glowing, and roll it some more.

4. The ends of the bead may need to be straightened so they're at a right angle to the mandrel. To achieve this, reheat the bead to just glowing. Hold the graphite paddle at the end of the bead, at a right angle to and lightly resting on the mandrel (see photo 3). With molten glass, it takes very little pressure to do this. Be careful; if you push too hard you'll lose the barrel shape you've made. Repeat for the other end of the bead if necessary.

5. Heat the bead to molten and glowing, almost to the point of losing the barrel shape. Lower the bead to the ridged surface of the marver, with the mandrel at a right angle to the ridges, and roll the bead on it, as shown in photo 4. As you make this first rotation, be sure to keep the mandrel oriented correctly, so that the beginning and end of the grooves line up properly with each other. Begin with a light pressure, increasing it as the bead cools and firms up. You can roll back and forth a few times to deepen the grooves.

6. The bead has cooled considerably, so return it to the hottest part of the flame; reheat the bead to almost glowing. Too much heat will cause the grooves to melt away.

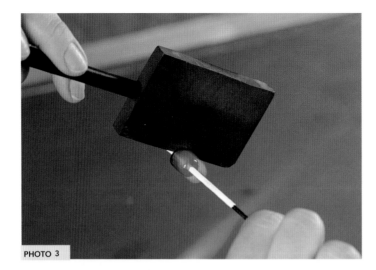

PHOTO 3

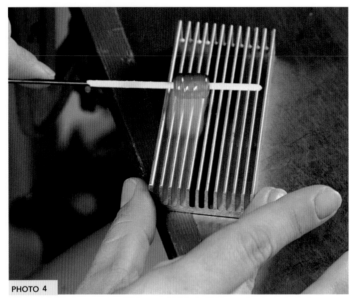

PHOTO 4

7. Once the bead is evenly heated, flame anneal it, then put the bead away in vermiculite. Once you're familiar with the process, consider rolling your next bead at an angle, or rolling it at two angles (reheat between rolls).

Glass Frit

Another way to decorate the surface of a bead is to use ground glass, or frit.

Frit is available in chunky pieces or in a more powdered form.

KIMBERLEY ADAMS

INSTRUCTIONS

1. Choose one or two colors of frit, and fill a nonfood metal teaspoon with each color. Arrange the handle of each spoon so you can easily pick it up and hold it under the flame later.

2. Now wrap a long bead—four or five times the width of the glass rod—on a mandrel. Use the graphite paddle to roll and move some glass out to the ends of the bead, as shown in photo 1. The ends of the bead should be slightly rounded. If the bead is pointed at the ends, it won't cool properly and it may not release smoothly from the mandrel later.

3. Pick up one of the spoonfuls of frit and hold it just below the flame, as shown in photo 2.

4. Heat the bead to glowing. Lower the molten bead to the spoon and roll it in the frit, picking up a layer of the ground glass (see photo 3).

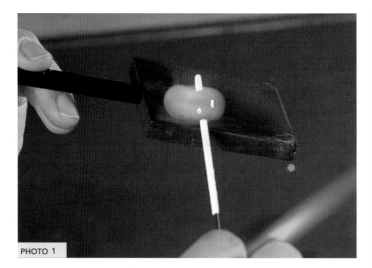

PHOTO 1

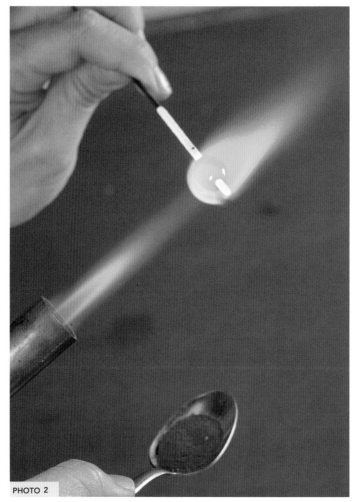

PHOTO 2

PHOTO 3

5. Bring the bead into the flame and allow the frit to heat and melt into the surface of the bead. The graphite paddle can be used to further smooth the frit.

6. Repeat steps 3 through 5 for additional colors of frit.

7. Be sure the bead is evenly heated before beginning the flame annealing process. Put the bead away to cool in the vermiculite-filled slow cooker.

Oval Wraps

This time you'll learn to add stringers— thin threads of glass—to a shaped oval bead. These strands of different-colored glass are used to decorate a bead in a variety of ways.

Kimberley Adams

KIMBERLEY ADAMS

INSTRUCTIONS

✖ **DESIGNER'S NOTE:**
Have your graphite paddle and needle nose pliers nearby.

1. To make a stringer, first heat a glass rod at the torch, holding and turning the rod first horizontally, then tipping the hot end up so the molten glass almost falls back onto the rod. Heat the rod's tip until you have a large pea-sized blob of hot glass, as shown in photo 1.

2. Bring the rod out of the flame and use the bent nose pliers to pinch a small bit of the molten glass (see photo 2). Begin pulling it slowly at first, so that the molten glass stretches out into a thread about the thickness of spaghetti. Don't pull too quickly, or you'll end up with a hairlike thread too thin to use. As you pull, you'll see the glass droop at first (see photo 3), then straighten out and become rigid as it cools and you continue to pull it, as shown in photos 4 and 5. It takes some practice to get the right thickness.

3. When you've pulled as much molten glass as you can, put the place where the stringer flattens out into the rod into the hottest part of the flame. Pull them apart slightly to separate them.

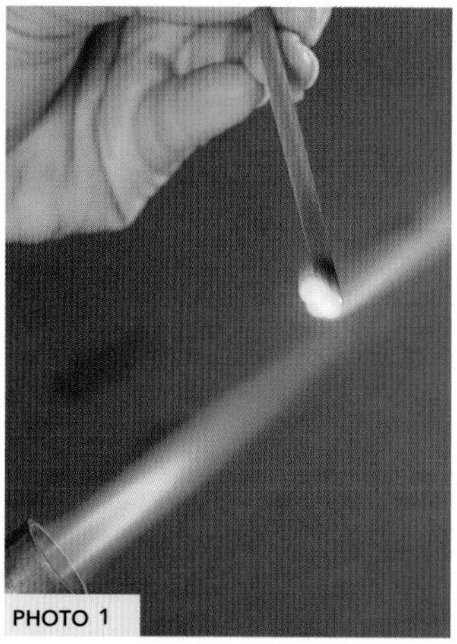
PHOTO 1

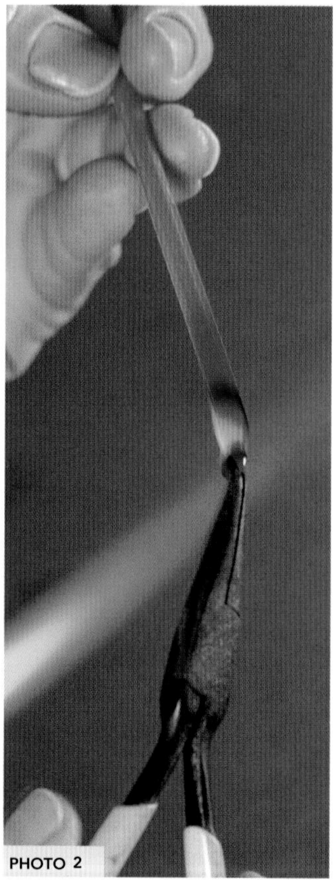
PHOTO 2

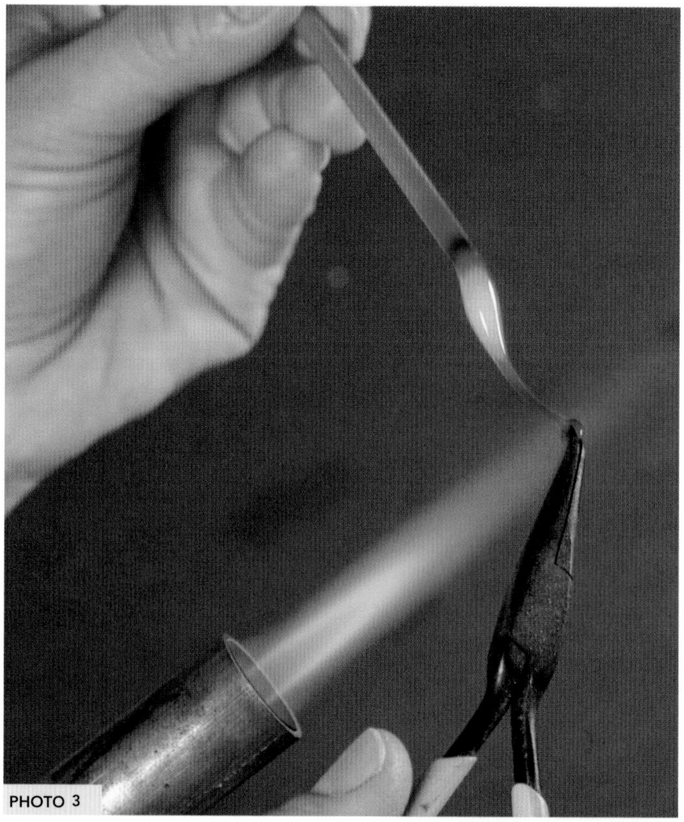
PHOTO 3

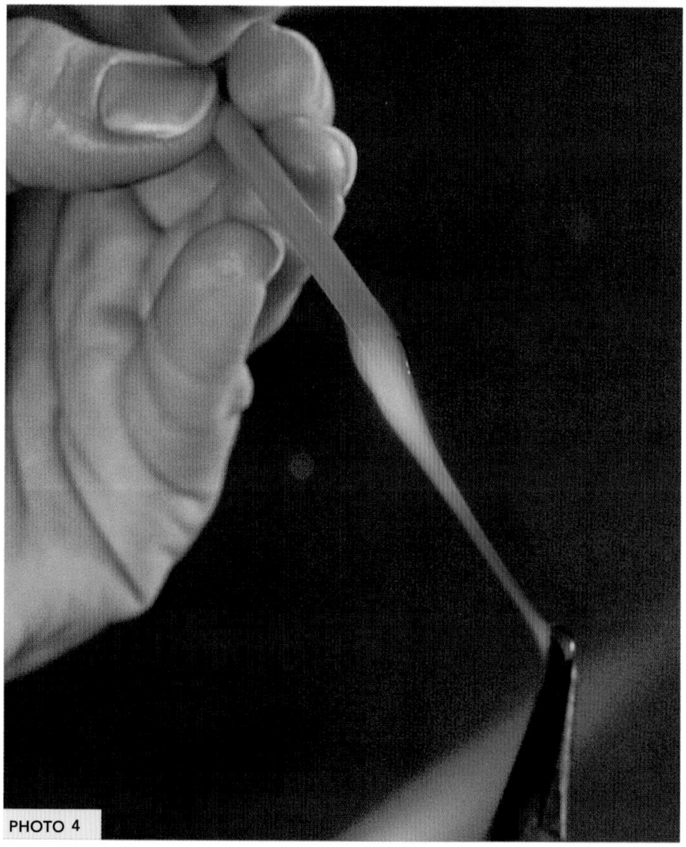
PHOTO 4

PHOTO 5

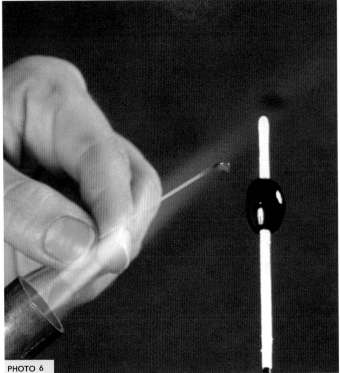

PHOTO 6

119

4. Lay the stringer down on the tabletop where you won't inadvertently touch it. The stringer will remain hot for only a minute or so.

5. Heat the glass rod to molten, and make an oval bead, as described in the Glass Frit bead project on page 116. Use the graphite paddle to round each end of the bead (remember, no pointed ends!).

6. Allow the bead to cool a bit by moving it to the end of the flame.

7. With your dominant hand, pick up the stringer and hold it underhanded, as shown in photo 6, so that its tip points up at an angle toward the flame. Hold the bead so it's just slightly under the flame.

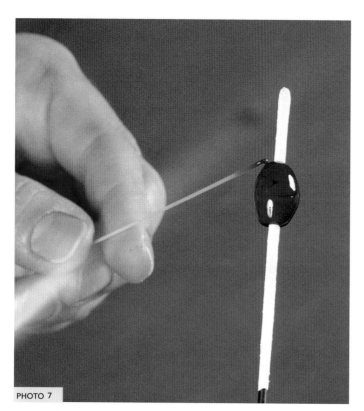

PHOTO 7

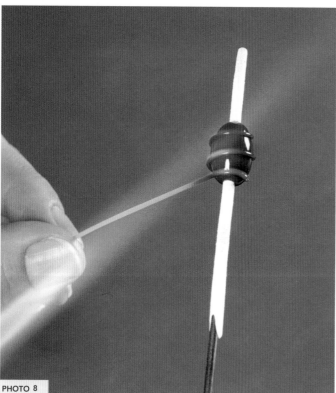

PHOTO 8

8. Heat the very tip of the stringer to molten and "glue" the end of the stringer to the end of the bead, near the tip of the mandrel. Referring to photo 7, bring the tip of the stringer up under the flame, inserting it into the place where the bead and the flame meet. Begin turning the bead away from you. This needn't be a quick motion, but you must keep up with wrapping the softening stringer around the bead.

9. Work your way down the bead in a spiral. To finish wrapping the stringer, bring the bead and connected stringer into the flame, then separate them, as shown in photo 8. The number of repetitions is up to you. You can leave room to add a second, or even third, stringer color on the bead.

10. The stringer can remain as a ridged texture on the bead, but it's important to let the stringer settle into the bead a bit by heating it in the warmer part of the flame. Bring the bead out of the flame and check its horizon so you can see that the stringer looks domed, rather than like a ball sitting on a flat surface. If the stringer hasn't been allowed to fuse well with the bead's surface, it may break off under impact.

You might want to try melting stringers flush into the surface of the bead. Use the graphite paddle to gently push the stringers into the surface; again, round the bead's ends with the paddle, if necessary, rather than letting them slope into thin, pointed ends.

11. Be sure that the bead is evenly heated before beginning the flame annealing process. Put the bead in hot vermiculite to cool.

Raked Barrels

Stringers are raked *(pushed and pulled)* around on the surface of the molten bead, creating a lovely marbleized pattern. The higher the contrast in the stringers, the more vibrant the effect.

KIMBERLEY ADAMS

INSTRUCTIONS

✖ **DESIGNER'S NOTE:** This project builds on your experience with the graphite paddle and with making stringers, two techniques introduced earlier.

1. Make two stringers (as demonstrated for the Oval Wrap on page117), each a different color, and set them near your dominant hand on the worktable. Heat and wrap molten glass on the mandrel to make a barrel shaped bead, as shown for the Groovy Bead on page 113.

2. Pick up the first stringer, and heat and wrap it in a spiral around the bead, leaving room for at least one more color stringer.

3. Choose a second color stringer and wrap it between the wraps of the first color, as shown in photo 1. Add another color or two if you like.

4. In order to melt the stringers but not lose the bead's shape, heat only the bead's surface by holding and turning it just at the top of the flame, as shown in photo 2. Allow the flame to touch just the lower side of the bead, rather than letting it shoot directly at the bead. Use the graphite paddle or flat marver to lightly push the stringers flush to the surface of the bead; see photo 3 on page 123.

5. Pick up the bead rake in your dominant hand. Heat one side of the entire length of the bead. Bring the bead out of the flame, and push the rake through the wraps, along the length of the bead's surface (see photo 4). Try not to push *into* the surface of the bead; instead, just scrape along the surface.

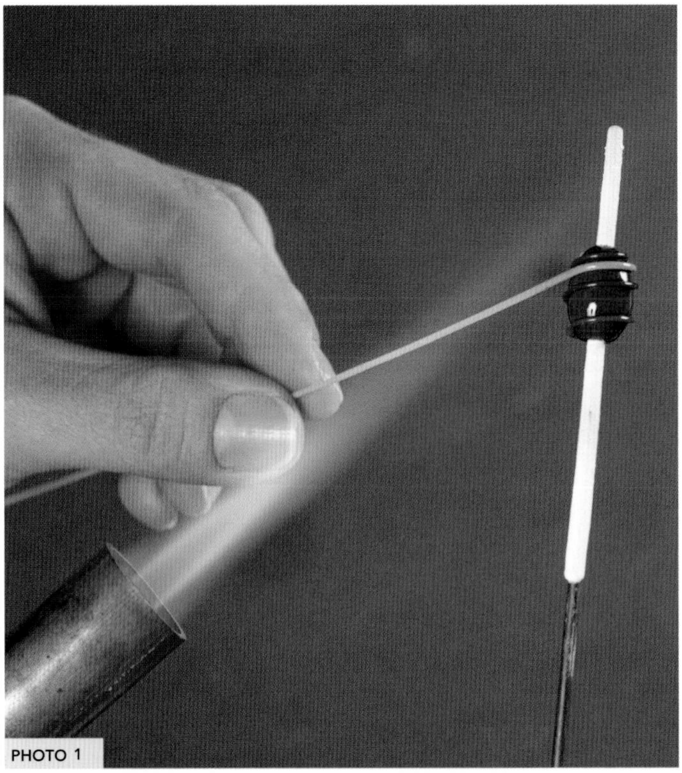
PHOTO 1

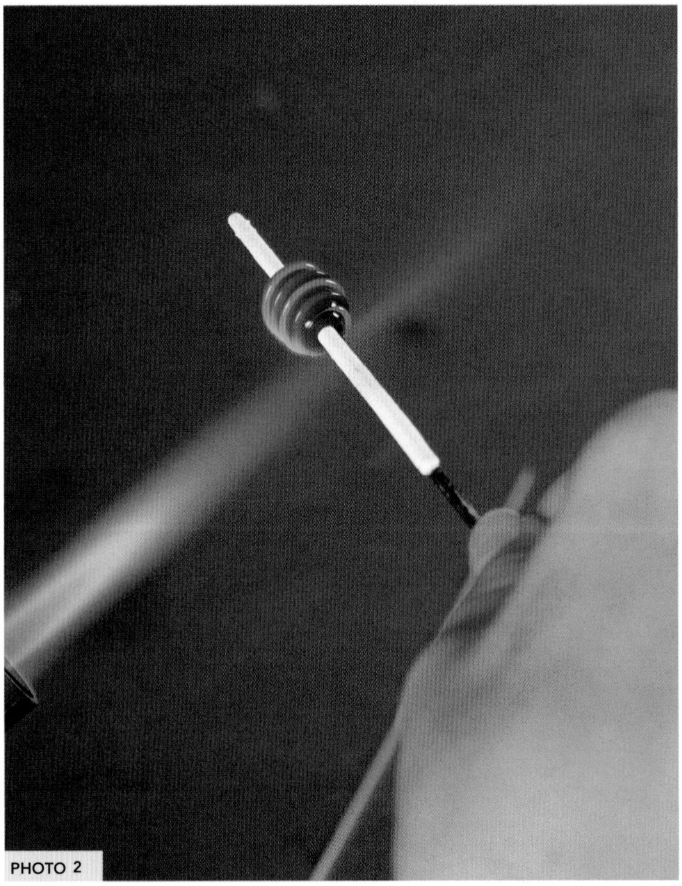
PHOTO 2

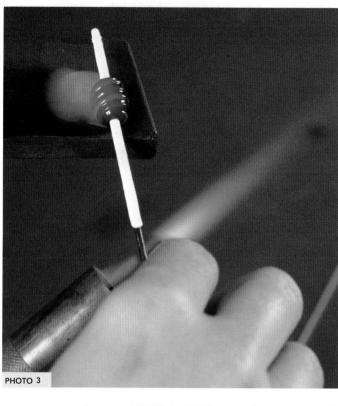

PHOTO 3

6. Turn the bead a little, and heat another section in the flame. Come out of the flame and repeat the raking. Cool the rake in the quenching bowl between pulls so that it doesn't get stuck in the glass. If the bead rake *does* get stuck, bring the bead and rake together out of the flame. Don't try to pull the rake out right away! The steel of the rake will cool more quickly than the glass and it will release from the glass after 10 seconds or so. At that point, try gently wiggling the rake a little to get it loose.

7. Reheat and reshape the bead back to a barrel shape.

8. Be sure the bead is evenly heated before beginning the flame annealing process, then put the bead in the slow cooker to cool.

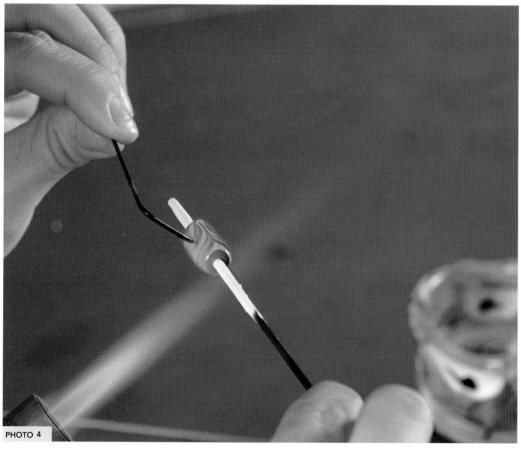

PHOTO 4

Metal Leaf
on Barrels

The effect of precious-metal leaf on glass can be as subtle or bold as you like.

KIMBERLEY ADAMS

INSTRUCTIONS

✳ DESIGNER'S NOTE: Different kinds of metal leaf can be layered on beads. You can experiment with layering the different leaf metals onto the bead for varied effects. Sheets of precious-metal leaf in silver, gold, or palladium can be purchased in most bead supply catalogs. The small sheet of metal leaf is light and diaphanous, and it will float away on the slightest breeze, so keep it weighted down—between its two sheets of protective paper—with a tool until you're ready to use it. Silver and gold are also available in heavier, more costly, foil sheets.

Use a pair of flat-tipped leaf tweezers to help you easily tear off small pieces. Each type of leaf has its own qualities; see step 3 for more information.

1. To make it easier to handle later, bend up one corner of the top sheet of the metal leaf's protective paper. Place the leaf, weighted with a tool, within reach of your dominant hand.

2. Wrap and shape a barrel bead, as described for the Groovy Beads on page 113.

3. Heat the bead to almost glowing, and bring it out of the flame. Using the flat leaf tweezers and just two fingers to lift the top paper, reach in and tear away a bit of leaf. Lay it on the surface of the hot bead and burnish the entire piece of leaf into the glass, as shown in photos

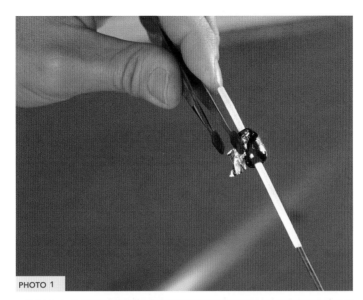

PHOTO 1

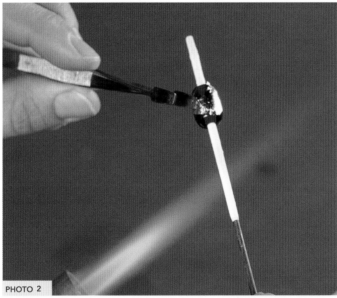

PHOTO 2

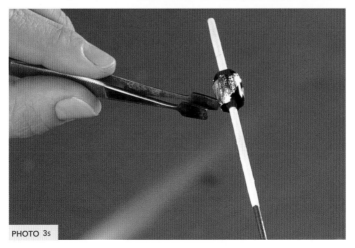

PHOTO 3s

1—3, with the flat end of the tweezers.

When using silver leaf, you have two options. In order for the silver to stay silvery, you must put the bead into the back flame so that it gets very little heat. The bead still needs to be heated evenly during the flame annealing process, but use a light touch with the heat! For a more subtle stain effect, melt the silver into the surface of the glass. The look of this method varies on different colors of glass.

With gold leaf, you'll use very little additional heat after burnishing the leaf on to the glass. Gold leaf must be heated so that it fuses with the glass, but it will disappear if too much heat is used. Take it slow by using the end of the flame, which is cooler.

Palladium leaf stays on the surface of the bead and won't melt into it. It can take a lot of heat and still stay metallic-looking. Palladium will show some iridescence if, when using an oxygen/propane torch, the oxygen in the flame is turned down, making a bushy flame.

4. Once the leaf is applied, be sure the bead is evenly heated, then begin the flame annealing process. Put the bead in the heated cooker to cool.

The soft, frosted look of etched beads is easily applied to any style of glass bead.

Etched Beads

INSTRUCTIONS

DESIGNER'S NOTE:

Etching acids eat into the surface of the glass and give it a soft, frosted look. They're available in some bead supply catalogs and from stained-glass suppliers. Ammonium bifluoride, available in liquid form, is simpler to use than the cream version. Be sure to use protective gloves and eyewear. Although etching can be used on just about any beads, don't use it on beads burnished with metal leaf—it will remove some or all the leaf. Cool and clean the beads before etching them. For best results, etch beads that were annealed in a kiln.

PHOTO 1

1. Make as many basic round beads as you want; for instructions, refer to pages 108-109 in the Basics section.

2. String the beads on heavy monofilament fishing line and knot both ends together. Lower the string into the bottle of etching liquid, making sure that the beads don't touch any part of the container (see photo 1).

3. Process the beads in the liquid for 15 minutes, or follow the manufacturer's directions.

4. Stir 3 tablespoons (15 g) of baking soda into a container holding 16 ounces (480 mL) of water. Lift the beads out of the acid, and lower them into the baking soda-water solution, which will neutralize the acid. Stir the beads with a plastic spoon to flush the acid from the holes. Rinse them well with cool water, and dry. The etching won't show until the beads are dried.

5. If you'd like to keep some areas of the bead shiny, use colored fingernail polish (it's easier to see where you've painted) as a resist. Apply the polish and let it dry, then process the beads in the acid. Remove the polish with an acetone nail polish remover. Rinse the beads again in cool water, then let dry.

KIMBERLEY ADAMS

Kimberley Adams

Making glass beads is like escaping to another world for me... a world of color, imagination, expression and, above all, peace and quiet. After more than 15 years in the corporate world, peace and quiet are something I cherish. Working as an incentive meeting planner in Chicago, my career took me to every corner of the world, from Des Moines to Beijing, and Phoenix to Madrid. My schedule was exciting and hectic, and it certainly didn't slow down after my marriage to my husband, Paul, and the arrival of our two children, Ian and Jordan. When I finally took the leap to be a full-time mother, I found myself fortunate to be with my children, yet I craved creative challenges. Through various attempts at self-expression, such as sewing and returning to college to earn a degree in fashion design, my true passion was sparked when I took my first glass bead making class. After that, I began to create beads into the wee hours of the "peaceful and quiet" morning!

Now that I've left Chicago's hectic pace, I call the mountains of western North Carolina home. Although my husband continued his career in advertising,

Asymmetrical Earring Pair,
2001. Left: ¾ in. (1.9 cm)
diameter; right: ⅜ in. (9.5 mm)
diameter sphere and cone.
Photo by Jerry Anthony

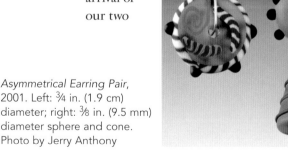

I was amazed at the opportunities open to me.

It's been seven years since we created our own business, marketing and selling my jewelry to galleries throughout the country. We also co-own Hand in Hand Gallery in Flat Rock, North Carolina, where I teach beadmaking; I also teach at John C. Campbell Folk School in Brasstown, North Carolina. Looking back, it seems quite scary, but at the time it never occurred to us to do anything else. We work harder sometimes than I think we ever have, but it never seems boring or meaningless. My mind is constantly challenged, I have time to be with my family, and, believe it or not, whenever things seem as hectic as when I lived in Chicago, I walk out to my studio, turn on the stereo, light the torch, and everything is peaceful and quiet again.

Vessel Necklace, 2001. Pendant: 1½ x 2½ in. (3.8 x 6.4 cm); bicones: 1 in. (2.5 cm); barrels and ovals: ¾ in. (1.9 cm); spheres: ½ in. (1.3 cm) and ⅝ in. 1.6 cm). Photo by Jerry Anthony

My Spiral Necklace and Bracelet, 2000. Necklace: 22 in. (55.8 cm); bracelet: 7 in. (17.8 cm). Photo by Seth Tice-Lewis

Lampworked Hollow Beads, Heather Trimlett, 2000. 1¾ in. (4.5 cm).
Photo by Melinda Holden

Hawaiian Lava, Alethia Donathan, 1999. From ¾ in. (1.9 cm) to 1 in. (2.5 cm). Photo by Hal Lum

Rose Tube Bead, Budd Mellichamp, 2001. 1⅜ x ⅜ x ⅜ in. (3.5 x 1 x 1 cm). Photo by Robert Overton

Hot Summer Fun Beads, Lucinda (Cindy) Brown, 2000. Left: ⅝ x ¾ x ¾ in. (1.6 x 1.9 x 1.9 cm); right: ⅞ x 1 x 1 in. (2.2 x 2.5 x 2.5 cm). Photo by Robert K. Liu

Borosilicate Beads, Amy Haftkowycz, 2001. Largest: 11.2 in. (3.8 cm). Photo by Steven Waskow

Red Window Bead, Larry Scott, 2000. 2 x $\frac{9}{16}$ x $\frac{9}{16}$ in. (5.2 x 1.4 x 1.4 cm). Photo by Roger Schreiber

Roman Glass Beads, Tracy Hildebrand, 2000. From $\frac{5}{8}$ x $\frac{3}{8}$ x $\frac{5}{8}$ in. (1.6 x 1 x 1.6 cm) to $\frac{5}{8}$ x $1\frac{1}{4}$ x $\frac{5}{8}$ in. (1.6 x 3.1 x 1.6 cm). Photo by Stewart Stokes

Temari, Emiko Sawamoto, 1999. 1 in. (2.5 cm). Photo by Rich Images

Shibori, Joel Park, 2001. ⅞ x ⅝ x ⅝ in. (2.2 x 1.6 x 1.6 cm). Photo by Shuzo Uemoto

Kaleidoscope, Deanna Griffin Dove, 2001. 1 x 1½ x ½ in. Photo by artist

Seaform, Budd Mellichamp, 2000. 1¾ x 1¹⁄₁₆ x 1¹⁄₁₆ in. (4.5 x 2.6 x 2.6 cm). Photo by Robert Overton

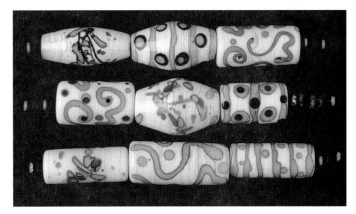

Turquoise on Ivory Beads, Tracy Hildebrand, 2000. From ⅜ x ¾ x ⅜ in. (1 x 1.9 x 1 cm) to 5/8 x 1 x ⅝ in. (1.6 x 2.5 x 1.6 cm). Photo by Stewart Stokes

Making the Most of Your Beads

Now that you've made some fabulous beads, how will you use them?
Beads can go literally anywhere: sewn onto handbags or tied into the
ends of your shoelaces. Perhaps you'll use them on the end of a light
switch chain, or even as a beaded fringe on a lamp shade or window
shade. The most common application, though, is to use them in
jewelry designs, whether necklaces, earrings, bracelets, or pins.
To get you started, here are some tips on what you'll need for
a finished piece of jewelry.

Design Decisions

When stringing your handmade bead into jewelry, the first decision to make is whether you want your bead to stand alone or to have company.

If your bead goes solo, pick out complementary stringing material and findings. You can keep a single bead in place by tying a knot on either side of the bead, then add more of your handmade beads on either side, a small distance from the first. Tie knots on either side of these beads, so your beads "float" along the length of the cord.

If your bead could use a little company, put a few beads on either side of it. Glass pony or crow beads work particularly well for this. Bring your bead to the bead store and experiment with different sizes, shapes, and colors of beads until you find the perfect combination.

Should you want the entire length of a necklace or bracelet to be beaded, you'll need filler beads. Filler beads are simply beads that won't detract from your origi-

1. Filler beads
2. Leather ends
3. Rattail
4. Beading thread
5. Needle nose pliers
6. Toggle clasps
7. Barrel clasps
8. Jump rings

nal handmade bead. You can work with just one type of filler bead, or experiment with several colors and shapes. Glass seed beads work well, as they are inexpensive and come in an astonishing variety of colors and sizes. You can string these beads in a pattern or put them all in a bowl and string them randomly. If your bead has a large hole, try stringing it on multiple strands of filler beads.

Wire, Chain & Cord

The most versatile way to wear and display your beads is to put them on some sort of stringing material, whether it's synthetic bead string, a simple wire chain made from silver or gold, or a piece of cord in leather, satin, or waxed linen or cotton. Tie a quick adjustable knot, or for a more finished look, add appropriate jewelry findings.

1. Bead tips
2. Lobster claws
3. Seed beads
4. Headpins
5. Jeweler's pliers
6. Accent beads
7. Leather cord
8. Wire cutters
9. Beading string

Findings

Findings is the catchall term for the range of jewelry-making bits and pieces that can turn your beads into wearable art.

A clasp, added to the ends of a cord or chain, allows you to open and close a necklace or bracelet, and there are many styles available. Be sure to choose one strong enough for the combined weight of your beads and stringing material.

Split rings are simple wire circles, available in several sizes, that can join different jewelry findings together. They look and work like a key ring.

Clamshells and bead tips are findings used to finish the ends of thinner stringing materials. Both hide the knot tied in the end of the string. A clamshell closes up around it, and a bead tip cups the knot in a hollow depression. To use these findings, put a dab of white craft glue on the end of the string, thread it through the clamshell or tip, and tie a sturdy knot. If you use a clamshell, close it up using small pliers. Attach either of these findings to the ends of a clasp by inserting the tab on the end through the ring of the clasp. Fold the tab down with a pair of pliers.

For thicker cords, you can use a clamp to attach the end to the clasp. There are several styles of clamps, but they all work the same way. Dab some white craft glue on the end of the cord, insert it into the clamp, and close the clamp with a pair of pliers. Then attach the ring of the clasp to the ring on the clamp.

Headpins are perfect for making your beads into earrings. A headpin is a straight piece of wire flattened on one end, like the head of a nail. Simply slip your bead onto the wire, make a loop at the top (with a round-nose, needle nose, or jeweler's pliers), and attach it to an earring wire! If the hole in your bead is too big and the bead slips off the end of the headpin, put a smaller bead (with a smaller hole) onto the headpin first. This bead will keep your handmade bead on the headpin.

To create earrings, there are many ready-made types of pierced and clasp-style (nonpierced) earring findings. For pins, and bracelets, there are dozens of pre-shaped wire pin styles, and you can even add beads to wire bracelet forms. All types of jewelry findings are widely available at bead shops and through catalog and online sales.

Beyond Jewelry

There's no need to limit your beads to just jewelry. Use your beads in place of buttons on a special sweater. String several of them onto gold wire, then coil the wire onto the base of a wine glass, for a special romantic touch. Embellish the zipper pull on your purse with a single, spectacular bead. If you let your imagination go, you'll soon be showing off your handmade beads in new and wonderful ways.

Acknowledgments

Thank you Spock, for your sweet company during the polymer clay photo shoot.

It's not often that we put together a book written with the expertise and creative efforts of a group of guest writers. We began from the premise that *Making Beautiful Beads* would feature the basic materials of glass, metal, fiber, and polymer clay, and then drew together the handmaking and writing talents of five special craftswomen to see it through. Thank you to these remarkable, indefatigable women, who each opened their working studios to us for a day while we photographed, poked about, and asked plenty of questions about their crafts and their lives.

With her on-the-ball assistance and advice, bead lover and editorial assistant Rain Newcomb was invaluable to this book. Thanks must also go to the staff at Chevron Bead and Trading Post, because they're always there with just the right finding and a laid back attitude; to Irene Semanchuk Dean, who helped out with additional technical assistance on the mysteries of the electronic bulletin board; and to Susan McBride, for the thoughtful care that made each image and page a beautiful experience. Finally, grateful thanks go to Evan Bracken, both for his steady, skillful hand and eye on each shot, and for the ready way he has shared his camera with me.

—*Suzanne Tourtillott, Editor*

Gallery Artists

GLASS

LUCINDA (CINDY) BROWN makes lampwork beads lovingly by hand. Look for her pawprint "signature" on them. Cindy Beads, 6240 Everett Court, Unit C, Arvada, CO 80004 http://www.cindybeads.com

ALETHIA DONATHAN, known for her "Hawaiian Lava" series, applies contemporary designs to the ancient skills and techniques of lampworking. Some of her beads reflect the natural beauty of the islands, others preserve their history. DACS Beads, 1287 Kalani Street, #102, Honolulu, Hawaii 96817 http://www.dacsbeads.com

DEANNA GRIFFIN DOVE found beads to be one of the constants in her life as she moved around Latin America, the Caribbean, Africa, and Europe. Beads have always been worn, handled, and exchanged. She loves making things that are so tiny yet so resonant of human values. 133 Hadley Rd, Dayton, OH 45419 <griffindove@mindspring.com>

AMY HAFTKOWYCZ has always loved glass. Creating her own unique little worlds inside of glass beads fulfills her need for creative expression beyond her wildest dreams. http://www.TheGlassMoon.com

TRACY HILDEBRAND combines two ancient crafts, lampworking beads and metal smithing, to create a contemporary line of silver and glass jewelry. Her work can be found in galleries around the Southeast. <traceworks@yahoo.com>

BUDD MELLICHAMP'S most well-known beads are from his "Sea Form" series, inspired by underwater life forms. Chimera Glass Works, 1520 Merry Oaks Ct., Tallahassee, FL 32303 <chimera@talweb.com>

JOEL PARK makes beautiful and thought-provoking glass beads by experimenting with different materials and exploring all of the possibilities of glass. 5302 Malu Place, Honolulu, HI 96816 <galleryeas1@cs.com>

EMIKO SAWAMOTO'S beads help her to rebel against the trend of conformity in her native culture. Each bead she makes is uniquely her own. Ruri Glass Studio, PO Box 9125, Berkeley, CA 94709 <emikoruri@earthlink.net>

LARRY SCOTT'S favorite part of the bead making process occurs when the entire bead and its design is at risk of total failure. Then the last drop of glass is added and the bead transforms itself into a miniature work of art. 5729 Woodlawn Ave. North, Seattle, WA 98103 http://www.larryscott.net

HEATHER TRIMLETT believes that life is too short not to enjoy it! Her bright beads are designed to make people smile. 12548 Melrose Place, El Cajon, CA 92021 http://www.heathertrimlett.com

POLYMER

DEBORAH ANDERSON fell in love with polymer clay in 1994. A year later, she founded the Southbay Polymer Clay Guild with Desiree McCrorey. 265 North 13th St., San Jose, CA 95112 <Maraha@aol.com>

DOROTHY GREYNOLDS brings a graphic design background to her work with polymer clay. She loves to layer Skinner blends and other small elements to create beautiful designs on the surface of the clay. Claywear, 5678 Eldridge Drive, Waterford, MI 48327 http://www.mdpag.org

PATRICIA KIMLE enjoys making beautiful things with polymer clay, but seeing others wearing and enjoying her work makes her even happier! 3222 Lettie St., Ames, IA 50014 http://www.kimledesigns.com

DESIREE MCCROREY found polymer clay in 1993 and hasn't put it down since! She loves the myriads of surface treatments and canework applications that polymer clay accommodates. Desired Creations, 2832 Orthello Way, Santa Clara, CA 95051 http://www.desiredcreations.com

CYNTHIA PACK creates boxes, sculptures, beads, and jewelry with polymer clay. Her favorite form of surface decoration is millefiori! <claycrazy1@yahoo.com>

SARAH NELSON SHRIVER'S beads are inspired by old textiles and the connections between science and nature. Color and spatial relationships are the foundation of her work. 8 Redding Way, San Rafael, CA 94901 <sshriver@dnai.com>

CYNTHIA TOOPS is inspired by Huichol Indian seed bead work and Roman micro-mosaics. She has been collaborating with glass bead maker Dan Adams since 1996. 6407 9th Avenue NE, Seattle, WA 98115 <cdbeads@earthlink.net>

DIANE W. VILLANO reproduces traditional beads on an exaggerated scale. She is awed at the skill and craftsmanship displayed by our bead artist ancestors. Foxon River Design, 1355 North High St., East Haven, CT 06512 <dianev_scpcg@yahoo.com>

METAL

SUSIE GANCH earned an M.F.A. at the University of Wisconsin-Madison and has been a metal-smith for seven years. She creates one-of-a-kind and limited-edition jewelry, and teaches workshops and classes throughout the U. S. <Susieganch@hotmail.com>

TIMOTHY A. HANSEN uses a variety of techniques to transform raw metals and stones into hand-crafted one-of-a-kind and limited-edition jewelry using gold, silver, platinum, copper, shakudo, shibuichi, mokume gane, and gemstones. TAH Handcrafted Jewelry, 305 N. Second Ave., PMB #131, Upland, CA 91786-6028 http://www.tah-handcrafted-jewelry.com

FAE MELLICHAMP works in a variety of metals. She uses textures and patinas to add depth and dimension to her work. Chimera Glass Works, 1520 Merry Oaks Ct., Tallahassee, FL 32303 <chimera@talweb.com>

PAT MOSES-CAUDEL has been working with wire for 18 years. She is a designer for Lapidary Journal and also creates workshops. Wild Poppy Designs, PO Box 5111, Richmond, CA 94806 http://www.members.aol.com/patmcaudel/2index.html

ERNEST P. NERI is inspired by ancient art and artifacts. His work is an attempt to communicate the feeling of humankind's existence through time. 121 Old Sachem's Head Rd., Guilford, CT 06437 http://www.havocmaker.com/artifact.htm

KRISTEN FRANTZEN ORR tries to capture and reflect light in every bead she makes, whether it is crocheted wire or glass. 1834 E. Inca Circle, Mesa, AZ 85203-2809 http://members.home.net/kfoartglass/

FELT

VICTORIA BROWN has been a felt-maker for more than 20 years and is a senior lecturer in textile fine art. 181 Main Road, Emsworth, Hampshire UK PO1O 8E2 <tosavage@lineone.net>

JEAN HICKS is a milliner /sculptor/teacher who has been working in felt for more than 10 years. PO Box 4394, Seattle, WA 98104 http://erraticahats.com

GERDA KOHLMAYR'S felt beads are a kind of meditation for her. Water and the artist's hands transform wool into the perfect sphere. Textil-Atelier Gerda Kohlmayr, A-3581 Kautzen, Tiefenbach 21, Austria <gerda.Kohlmayr@utanet.at>

LEENA SIPILA Though I work as an arts and crafts teacher, at home I relax by felting and planning for the development of my institute's felt department.

YUMIKO YANAGIHARA lives in the Japanese Alps. She is very happy to follow a simple, holistic lifestyle. She has returned to appreciating and recognizing the simple gifts that are received from nature, and is making a life surrounded by things she grows and makes with her own hands. 1-276 Kuwanoyama, Honkawane-cho, Haibara-gun, Japan 428-0413